Glennyce … angels and near-death … the world. Highly experienced in the media, she has made many appearances on TV and radio. She lives in Manchester, UK.

By the same author:

Saved by the Angels

An Angel at My Shoulder

Children and Angels

Angels and Miracles

TEEN ANGEL

True Stories of Teenage Experiences of Angels

GLENNYCE S. ECKERSLEY

RIDER BOOKS
R

RIDER

LONDON · SYDNEY · AUCKLAND · JOHANNESBURG

For Janice O'Gara, with love.

1 3 5 7 9 10 8 6 4 2

First published in Great Britain in 2003 by Rider,
an imprint of Ebury Press, Random House,
20 Vauxhall Bridge Road, London SW1V 2SA

Random House Australia (Pty) Limited
20 Alfred Street, Milsons Point, Sydney,
New South Wales 2061, Australia

Random House New Zealand Limited
18 Poland Road, Glenfield,
Auckland 10, New Zealand

Random House South Africa (Pty) Limited
Endulini, 5A Jubilee Road,
Parktown 2193, South Africa

The Random House Group Limited Reg. No. 954009

Papers used by Rider are natural, recyclable products made from wood grown in sustainable forests.

Printed and bound in Great Britain by Bookmarque Ltd, Croydon , Surrey

A CIP catalogue record for this book
is available from the British Library

ISBN 1-8441-3038-X

Contents

Acknowledgements

I am so very grateful to all the special people, who guide me through the process of writing a book. Firstly Judith Kendra, the Publishing Director of Rider Books, deserves a huge thank you for her continuing support and confidence in me. To Sue Lascelles, my editor, I send heartfelt thanks for her guidance and expert advice and to my friend David Lomax for his valued contribution. Thank you to my circle of friends, including the 'Wednesday Women', for their help with research, emotional support and encouragement. Thanks to Stella Morris and her staff at Sweetens bookshop. As ever, I am deeply indebted to my family for all their help, especially, Gillian, Michael, Rachel and Ed, who cheerfully offer sound practical help and advice throughout.

To the generous contributors who willingly gave me their accounts, I give thanks most sincerely. I am deeply grateful, for without them there simply would not be a book. They are: Isabelle Adams, Miriam Aitken, Rev Beryl Allerton, Beverley Bass, Connie Benetz, Nicola Bowen, Barbara Brophy, Chris Burgess, Judi Chsysanthom, Carol Dickson, Helen Doyle, Alison Ferrier, Megan Foster, Jenny Fox, Barbara Gardiner, Joanne Gardiner, Janet Gittins, Ann-Marie Gomez, Joan Goodwin, Martha Goodwin, Emma Green, Frank Harlie, Michelle Hodgkinson, Linda Hughes, Catherine Norma Hughes, Janet Jepherson, Patricia Jolly, Margaret Jones, Lisa Kennedy, Samantha King, Amanda and Thomas Lloyd, Sophia Lucas, Stephanie Lumb, Ian Maddox, Barry May, Mary McHugh, Nadine Mills, Dr. H. Moolenburgh, Toby Newton, Melissa Pengier, Helen Prosser, Katherine Overton, Rev J. Rainer, Angela Rigby, Joyce Roberts, Amy Sheldon, Gillian Smith, Ysanne Spevack, Ellie Taylor, Elizabeth Tudoran, Jessica Walters, Vanessa Watson, Lesley White and Lynne Marie Zamir. My thanks also go to Sara, Abby, Sue, Robert, Laura, Bethany, Mee, Gemma and Clare.

Every effort was made to obtain permission to reproduce stories from the USA publication, *National Enquirer*.

Introduction

Are you searching for something special from life? Do you want to make your mark, take a stand or find a sense of direction and purpose? Today many of us appear to have everything we could possibly want – money, possessions, a degree of freedom – but we can still feel as though we're missing something. And though it may seem to others that we've got it easy, the world isn't always a friendly place. Exams, romantic problems, trouble at home – life can be hard going. (And that's without even mentioning global issues such as war, politics and the environment.)

So it's no wonder that more and more people today are being drawn to the paranormal, either as a way of escaping from everything or as a means of making sense of it all. Life-after-death and other-world experiences fascinate many of us – consciously or subconsciously – perhaps because we want to be sure that another world really does exist and that we are not alone in this one after all.

The popular appeal of things mystical and magical is reflected in the success of television programmes and films such as *Buffy the Vampire Slayer, Dark Angel, Sabrina the Teenage Witch* and *Charmed,* to name just a few. Films such as those in the *Lord of the Rings* trilogy have also been hugely influential in encouraging our current fascination with magic and the supernatural.

Even little kids appear to be anxious to believe that there is 'something else' besides this world. In the film *Harry Potter and the Philosopher's Stone* there is a very moving scene in which Harry gazes into a magic mirror and sees the reflection of his dead parents. Harry realises that he is not alone, that his parents are watching over him and loving him still, from the next life. And this scene is not as far-fetched as some might think. The respected physician and researcher Dr. Raymond Moody discovered that when people sit in a darkened room, gazing into a mirror, many are able to see their deceased relatives. He has written a book about his research called *Life After Life*.

Booksellers report a huge interest in books about witchcraft, wicca and magic spells, and in the last couple of years, a plethora of titles has been published on these subjects. But it is not only witches and wizards that are gaining in popularity; there is a growing fascination with angels too. Books on the subject are literally 'flying off the shelves' (if you'll pardon the pun).

There is, however, one very important point to ponder. While witchcraft is a fast-growing religion these days, most modern witches would not claim to be anything other than ordinary human beings with ordinary human powers. Angels, however ... well, that's a different matter altogether. Angels – those most magical of beings – are definitely not mortal creatures. Nevertheless, they certainly exist. And an encounter with one of them could happen at any time, because the fact is that they influence all our lives.

The stories in this book are about encounters with angels, and they are all true (although one or two names have been changed to protect people's privacy). They show that angels really are watching over us, and they suggest that a particularly close bond exists between angels and teenagers. Angels have appeared at the most unlikely of times and in the most unlikely of places, sometimes inspiring music and creativity, sometimes even saving lives, but always providing protection and guidance. As well as being exciting, the world is also a tough place sometimes, and it can be very reassuring to know that your very own guardian angel may be standing close by you right now …

Chapter 1

Angels and Music

Angel voices ever singing round thy throne of light,
Angel harps forever ringing rest not day or night.

Francis Pott

Music is often referred to as the universal language, as you don't need to speak any particular language to understand or enjoy music. It binds people together with its beauty, inspiration and energy. All sorts of feelings and memories can be encapsulated in a melody, which may express how we feel much more succinctly than words. Lovers have their special songs, and weddings and funerals are often remembered for the music played. Music unites people in a shared experience and a sense of common cause. Anyone who has ever played in a band or been part of the crowd at a concert will have experienced the power of music first-hand. I recall watching the Commonwealth Games in Manchester in the summer of 2002 and remember how the music stirred my heart when an athlete stood on the winner's podium and their national anthem was played. With tears of joy and an overwhelming sense of national pride, the athlete's compatriots sang along with the music.

Many composers, classical and pop, will tell you that music often simply arrives in their head just like a gift or a spiritual email.

These people seem to be able to 'tune in' to music in the ether, as it were. Music also links heaven and earth, acting as a bridge for the angels. It is widely believed that because humans have free will, angels need our co-operation if they are to contact and help us. Music is one medium through which they can do this. In my book *Children and Angels* you'll find the very moving story of teenage brothers, Michael and Steve. They were very close and shared the special bond of music. After Michael sadly died, he appeared to his brother one morning and told him that music in heaven was indescribably beautiful and quite unlike any he had ever experienced on earth.

The following stories illustrate connections with angels through music. It's no coincidence that angels are so often depicted playing harps or trumpets. The harp is a particularly sweet and soothing instrument. In the United States there is a group of harpists who play to very sick people and those dying in hospices. Their music consoles and comforts, bringing a sense of peace to those in need. In the Bible, too, David played his harp for King Saul to ease his bouts of depression. A person who has an angelic or near-death experience will often relate that their vision was accompanied by angels playing beautiful music. Bells that make an ethereal tinkling sound are frequently mentioned, suggesting links with ancient temple bells. And stories of angels joining in while music is being played or when people are singing are not uncommon. Seemingly, angels wish to add to the atmosphere, especially when it's of a spiritual nature.

There are many tales of angels accompanying people who are playing or singing – be it in a church congregation, in a rock band or alone in their room for their own amusement. Let's begin with the story of Ray, a talented young musician who found inspiration where he wasn't expecting it.

It's every band's dream to tour the United States. Ray's band was no exception. And they were over the moon when their tour turned out to be a great success. The social scene that went along with it was pretty exciting, and, of course, they encountered a lot of drug-taking in the clubs they went to. However, talking to young people led them to some surprising conclusions. They came to believe that the young people they met were actually searching for something spiritual.

After the tour, the band discussed this issue and decided that they would like to make an album of club-friendly, spiritual music. Many aspiring young musicians had given them CDs and tapes on the tour. With their new idea in mind, the band started to listen to them.

One tape – of rather poor quality – was a recording of a small group of Canadian teenagers who had got together for a singing session. Their song was called 'Cilegna', which Ray soon realised was 'angelic' backwards. As they listened to the tape, the band suddenly had a huge surprise. Joining in the song at one point was a huge chorus of exquisite voices. It gave them all shivers: no earthly singers could possibly have made that sound – the volume and scale of the voices were beyond description. A heavenly choir had joined the small group of teenagers, and clearly it was enjoying the session as much as the young people. This unexpected discovery gave Ray and his band just the inspiration that they had been searching for.

Why she ever agreed to take part in the concert Laura will never know. Her teacher was pressurising her to play in it and, deep down, she did feel that if she had the talent she should use it. Which was all well and good until the day of the concert came around ...

Laura had played the flute for many years – since infant school to be precise. Her talent was obvious and she loved to play with the school orchestra. Hoping to study music at university, Laura studied hard and was looking forward to the future. The main problem came when she was asked to play solo. That was when her nerves really got the better of her. The end-of-term concert was to be special. A school orchestra from the continent was taking part and a city centre hall had been hired. All in all, it was to be a big occasion in every sense of the word.

As she practised in her bedroom, Laura felt the panic rising. Her fingers simply would not obey her. She simply did not know what she was going to do. It was far too late to pull out of the concert, but she was certain that she was going to make a fool of herself. She sat sipping a cup of tea, staring at the music, as despair began to overwhelm her and the tears started to flow. Not one for praying, she nevertheless found herself saying, 'Please God, help me.'

Finishing her cup of tea, she lifted her flute and began to play. This time a feeling of calm flooded through her as the beautiful music filled the room. Then, incredible as it seemed, she became aware of voices singing the melody as she played. Unable to believe her ears, she jumped from her chair and glanced around the room, but she was completely alone. She ran downstairs, but the house was deserted; no one else was at home. She slowly climbed the stairs back to her room feeling totally confused.

Once more Laura started to play and once more the beautiful voices joined in. This time her feeling of calm was accompanied by sensations of great happiness. Something unworldly was taking place ... Feelings of love and support surrounded her, and she knew instinctively that angels were with her. There was no need to fear the concert; she would not be alone. For what felt like hours but was in fact only moments, Laura played with this wonderful accompaniment. It was a life-changing experience.

The concert was a triumph. Laura managed to control her nerves and she herself played like an angel. Laura's future will be filled with music. She never doubts for a moment that angels and music are very closely connected.

★ ★ ✶

The illness engulfed Gemma with such speed it took everyone by surprise – even the medical staff. Arriving home from a friend's house one evening, Gemma complained of feeling unwell. Within an hour she was so dreadfully ill that an ambulance was called and she was admitted to hospital. Her parents could scarcely take in what the doctor told them: 'Gemma has meningitis.' Their world was turned upside down. Their daughter, only just fourteen years old, was dangerously ill. How they would get through the next few hours they had no idea.

What about Gemma? How was she facing those terrible hours? She says that most of the journey to hospital was a blur. Only the white coats and bright lights of the hospital are imprinted on her memory. It was difficult for her to make sense of what was said to her – and then suddenly there was nothing but blackness. Sounds and sights had faded away.

What happened next will stay with Gemma forever. The first thing she was aware of was a soft white light penetrating the blackness. As this grew in intensity she recalls a sense of movement. It was, she says, like being on a train that moves slowly initially, then increases in speed until you feel you are being swept along. This journey appeared timeless. She was aware of stars and colours swirling in the wonderful light and was enveloped by feelings of well-being and love. She felt absolutely no fear.

What amazed Gemma the most, however, was the music. It was like none she had ever heard before and was almost impossible to describe. It was a harmony of beautiful sound, incorporating every instrument you could imagine and several that you could not. One sound that particularly impressed her was 'like soft gentle wind chimes and tiny bells'. It was so wonderful she wanted it to go on forever, but she became aware that it was in fact fading. The sensation of speed had gone into reverse and she was conscious of travelling backwards. Although the following days in hospital remain for Gemma a blur, her wonderful experience of music is still crystal clear.

Eventually Gemma returned home, much to the relief of her worried family. Sitting with her mother one morning, she told her what had she had seen and heard on that first night in hospital. At once her mother recognised it as a near death experience. Gemma had never heard of such a thing and was astonished to think that she had almost reached heaven. 'I wish I could have a recording of that music,' she told her mum. 'Then everyone would then believe in life after death!'

★ ★ ★

I must admit, I know nothing about jungle music – or 'breakbeat', as it's also called. I'm pretty sure, though, that many of you will know exactly what it is. The person largely responsible for introducing and promoting this music in Britain was a young man named Vinni Medley. A talented singer-songwriter, Vinni had played in California at many open mike sessions before leaving the Californian music scene to return to his native London. There, embarking on a new direction, he founded a record label that gloried in the name of Botchit and Scarper. A talented DJ with a charismatic personality, he successfully managed music events. Vinni was greatly admired and loved by everyone who knew him. Around him was a close group of friends, bonded together by their love of music.

I recently met one of these friends, a girl called Mee. She is also a very talented musician – a violinist and professional composer who these days works mainly with computers and samplers. If this was not talent enough, she also writes books. Mee is a very smart, warm and engaging person. This is the story she told me.

One Christmas, a couple of years ago, Vinni was enjoying a DJing session when he was suddenly struck by a very painful headache. He continued to suffer from headaches like this periodically for a year or more. Eventually he realised that he needed to have the problem investigated, and it was discovered that he had a brain tumour. He was told that there was little hope of recovery.

In someone so young and so full of life, this death sentence seemed especially tragic. Mee, like Vinni's other friends, found it difficult to accept. It all seemed so unreal.

One evening Mee and Vinni were chatting on the phone. For those few moments everything appeared to be normal. Later that night, Mee had a vivid dream. In it, Vinni appeared and she felt a strong feeling of love for him. He told her that he loved her and that she must remember him through his music. The following day, Mee learned that Vinni had in fact died during that night.

Vinni's family friends planned a funeral with a difference – an irreverent, upbeat service, featuring rock music. At one point in the service, the CD player started to jump inexplicably. For Vinni's friends this was highly significant, as 'scratch' techniques were part of Vinni's signature as a DJ. After the funeral, Mee told the group about her dream. She said she had felt that it was Vinni saying goodbye. To the astonishment of everyone, they discovered that many of them had experienced a similar lucid dream. As they discussed their dreams, they realised that Vinni was also urging them to remember him through his music. The wonderful CD of Vinni's music that was produced as a result is called *Forever Young*. As a result of this he will indeed never be forgotten.

Several strange and inexplicable events have happened to Vinni's friends since his death. One day Martin Love, Vinni's partner in Botchit and Scarper, was driving along the motorway listening to the radio. The car stereo was pre-tuned to Radio 1, the only station he ever listened to when driving. Suddenly there was interference, the sound crackled and the song being played was replaced by music from the album *Forever Young*. At end of the track, the radio presenter's voice revealed that this was a pirate radio station. Further crackling followed and the radio reverted to Radio 1, completely unaided!

Many of Vinni's friends have continued to have significant dreams and have experienced other forms of communication. Darrin was Vinni's closest friend. One evening, alone in his flat, he heard footsteps and felt Vinni's presence very strongly. A little later, his tape recorder switched itself on by itself. Mee told me that all of Vinni's friends have found these experiences to be positive.

To them, they that suggest that Vinni is happy in his new-found freedom.

★ ★ ★

Music is so much part of the fabric of our lives often we have only to hear a particular tune or song and we are immediately catapulted to the person or place it represents for us. Weddings frequently contain that emotional moment when the bride and groom have 'their special song' played. (Incidentally, it often seems to be Robbie Williams singing 'Angel'.) Similarly, a piece of music can bring someone close when we miss them and comfort us.

This was certainly true for Megan. When she was just sixteen years old, her mother died. As you can imagine, the family was overcome with grief. Megan and her younger brother felt completely bereft, and their poor father, grieving himself, had no idea how to comfort them. No one quite knew how to cope, but as Megan was an intelligent and practical girl she automatically took on the role of sorting out the household chores. She organised a rota for shopping and cleaning, making the day-to-day running of the house easier to manage. Nevertheless, she still missed her mum – and her mum's music – dreadfully.

Singing had been played a huge part in the life of Megan's mother. She had been a keen choir member and also an enthusiastic participant in the local amateur dramatic society. They often produced musicals, which the whole family enjoyed. Megan recalls that her mother's favourite song was 'Memories', a beautiful haunting melody which she would sing frequently at home.

Three years passed, and one day Megan's father asked if they could have a family conference. Megan and her brother had a pretty good idea what this meeting would be about. For several months now, Dawn, a friend of their father's, had been a regular visitor to the house, and the relationship appeared to be serious. And they were right: Megan's father wanted their permission to marry Dawn. Naturally, Megan and her brother felt very emotional about this prospect, but they liked Dawn very much and they wanted their father to be happy. However, this was not to be the greatest challenge facing them. It transpired that their father had been promoted, and as a result they would have to move house. The shock of leaving behind all that was familiar to them, including their friends, was a dreadful blow. Megan and her brother had no idea how they would cope with this on top of having lost their mother so recently.

The wedding was a small, personal and happy occasion. Everyone enjoyed it and, in spite of the planned move, the future didn't seem so bleak on that day. But when, several weeks later, a large furniture van pulled up outside the house the full impact of what was happening hit Megan and her brother. The drive to their new home was long and miserable, and it rained heavily all the way. Nevertheless, the new house looked OK, and their father took them all out for dinner, saying they would simply put up the beds that night and face the unpacking in the morning. The mood lightened a little as they enjoyed a pizza and chatted about exploring the neighbourhood. As they walked home, Dawn took Megan's hand, saying, 'You know, it doesn't matter where you live, your mother will always be with you.' Megan felt a rush of warmth and love for Dawn and gave her a thank-you hug.

Eventually the family retired to bed, but for Megan sleep simply would not come, and after an hour or so she sat up in bed. Not wanting to disturb anyone, she turned on her radio very quietly.

From it came the familiar, well-loved strains of 'Memories'. Megan listened in awe, Dawn had been right. Surely this was a sign that her mother would always be with her.

It came upon the midnight clear
That glorious song of old
From angels bending near the earth
To touch their harps of gold.

Edmund Hamilton Sears

It does seem logical that angel music might be heard more frequently in a spiritual setting, such as a church where people are worshipping, and I have heard several stories of this kind. One particularly lovely one comes from a church in Leicester called Holy Apostles. Peter Kitchen, Trevor Kirk and Shirley Mullholland were three very talented young people who belonged to the church. Peter wrote music and played the guitar, Trevor played the mandolin and Shirley sang soprano, and each Sunday morning they would perform together for the congregation.

One Wednesday evening Peter set off for church to meet his two friends for a rehearsal of a piece he had just written. He was thinking about what an ordinary day it had been and how it would cheer him up to play his guitar and sing.

The rehearsal went well and they all enjoyed Peter's song, which was entitled 'Standing in Your Prescience'. That particular night Shirley couldn't stay as long as usual. Saying her goodbyes, she left the church. Peter and Trevor played on, accompanying themselves as they sang. Then Peter suddenly became aware of other voices. For a moment he thought Shirley had joined them, but he knew for certain that she had left – he had seen her go through the door. The voices swelled and now Trevor also noticed the amazing sound. Looking for a logical explanation, they both put down their instruments, telling each other that the sound must be the result of an echo or some other technical trick. They could see for certain that they were the only two people in the church. But the singing continued. According to Peter, it was 'like a little glimpse of heaven'.

Excitedly they told the vicar about this amazing event when he returned from a meeting later that evening. They found the incident hard to relate or to explain. The vicar, however, said that he had experienced exactly the same phenomenon a few years earlier, but he had kept the incident to himself. When they compared notes it seemed that there was no doubt about it. On this occasion too the angels had decided to join in the heavenly music.

* * *

The death of someone you love is probably the most painful experience you will ever have to cope with. When that person is also very young there is the added dimension of how much life they have missed. And then there is the fact that you will also miss seeing them grow through life's many stages.

This is how Janet feels, having lost her son, Andrew, in a car accident in his late teens. Two years later Janet and her family are still struggling to come to terms with their loss. Andrew was much loved by his family and friends. It appears that everybody who met him warmed towards him, and he is dreadfully missed. Music was a large part of his life. He played in a band, composed and loved listening to music. Whenever he was alone in his bedroom the sound of it would fill the house. One of his favourite pieces of music was 'Angel', sung by Robbie Williams. This song was, then, an obvious choice for his very moving funeral.

After the funeral, Janet was lying in bed in the early hours of the morning with very little chance of being able to sleep. Suddenly she heard music coming from Andrew's room. Slipping out of bed she went to the room, baffled and curious. On entering she realised with a start that the music centre was playing 'Angel'. As if in a trance, she walked across to the tape deck. Standing there, she looked in the large bedroom mirror, fully expecting to see the reflection of her son, so powerful was the sensation of his presence. The song ended and the digital display flashed the poignant word 'goodbye'.

Janet tried, of course, to think of a logical explanation. Perhaps the music centre had been pre-set – but surely not for the early hours of the morning. The track was not at the start of the tape, and so the tape had come on in the middle. And why that particular song? Janet found it all very moving and also thought-provoking. There was no logical explanation when the phenomenon happened again. Indeed, it happened in all twice more – once during the evening and once when Janet and a friend were having a morning coffee in the kitchen Each time the word 'goodbye' appearing after the song had finished.

Knowing how much music meant to Andrew, it seems logical that this would be his chosen medium through which to communicate. However, Andrew's two brothers are very sceptical. They believe there is a logical explanation for all this. Janet also has her doubts. I can understand that completely. However, this is not the first time I have heard of such an experience, and it's not the only one in this book. I hope that, whatever they choose to believe, the music itself will always bring them comfort and warm memories.

For young people in the Western world it must be very difficult to imagine what life under war conditions is like. But many people alive today can still remember the Second World War and its associated miseries, and some of them have amazing stories to tell. Shony Alex Braun was a teenager during the 1939–45 war. Today he is grandfather living happily in California, but he clearly recalls the amazing wartime incident that saved his life.

As an inmate of a concentration camp he was miserable, frightened and starving. His young life appeared to be hanging by a thread, dependent on the whim of his captors. One day an SS guard came into the camp and asked if anyone could play the violin he was carrying. The commandant would give food to anyone who could play for him. Shony had not seen a violin since he was a child, but put his hand up, desperate to get something to eat. Two older men also raised their hands. All three men were marched before the commandant and ordered to play.

It was terrifying. The commandant looked very stern. He was dressed from head to toe in black leather and accompanied not only by guards but also by a fierce, large dog. The atmosphere was extremely tense as the first man was ordered to play. The elderly man took the violin and played quite beautifully a very sweet song. 'That was terrible,' the commandant barked and ordered the guards to kill him. In horror the other two watched as the poor man was beaten to death before their eyes. The second man was so terrified when it came to his turn that he could not keep his fingers from trembling on the violin. He found it hard to produce a single note. This man suffered the same fate as the first.

At this point Shony felt physically sick. He knew only too well that he had not played the instrument since he was a small child, and then, of course, it had been a small child's violin. The guard thrust the large violin into his hand and ordered him to play. His mind went a complete blank and he had no idea what to do. At this point he felt a powerful force take hold of his hands. His fingers were pressed onto the strings and the bow gripped by an invisible hand covering his. To his astonishment the most beautiful music poured from the violin, which Shony recognised as the Blue Danube waltz. He had never, ever, played that piece of music before, and he knew with certainty that God had sent an angel to guide his hands. When the sound of the last note died away, the commandant grudgingly gave the order for him to be given food. Shony's life had quite literally been saved by an angel playing the violin!

Shony's story is amazing and moving – and, one might think, unique. I have, however, encountered many stories of people being helped to produce music by unseen hands. For one eleven-year-old girl it was not a matter of life and death, although she was in a state of terror. Norma had just moved from primary to grammar school – not always an easy change.

Norma loved music, but she soon she came to dread the music lessons at her new school. The music teacher was a bully who appeared to take pleasure in embarrassing the girls. She pounced on their weaknesses and punished them with a rap on the knuckles. Norma's first distressing encounter with her happened at the very first music lesson she attended. The girls were lined up and one by one told to find and play 'middle c' on the piano. Norma had never played a piano in her life and had not the faintest idea where she might locate middle c. Trembling she approached the piano. Of course, she failed to play the note, and was subjected to verbal abuse and a whack.

The year went on, with Norma and her friends dreading each music lesson – particularly when it involved sight-reading. Rather than a pleasure, music became torture. So you can imagine how Norma dreaded the end-of-year music exam. To add to her growing fear, Norma found out, to her horror, that it was to take place in the corner of a room already occupied by another class. They could watch with wide eyes as the humiliation unfolded.

The day of the exam finally came. Standing in line outside the classroom, the girls trembled at the thought of what was to come. Each girl had to sing, sight-read and compose a piece of music. An exacting task in any circumstances, but in front of so many people ... And, of course, the teacher was, as ever, only too ready to pounce. Eventually it was Norma's turn to be examined. Her legs turned to jelly and her mouth was so dry she knew for certain not a single note would emerge from it. She found herself saying softly, 'Please God, help me.' She approached the teacher, who handed her a piece of sheet music and told her to sing.

When she opened her mouth Norma was astounded to hear the most beautiful voice emerge. 'Where is this coming from?' she wondered. This amazing feat was followed by an ability to sight-read the music perfectly! She had no idea how this could be. For an average singer and a poor sight reader, it was nothing short of a miracle. She finished the exam in a dream-like state and passed with flying colours. Indeed, her teacher commented, with a note of surprise in her voice, 'That was excellent' – high praise from one so severe in her judgements.

Relieved that the ordeal was over, all Norma could think of was her miraculous escape. She was convinced that someone or something had come to her rescue. She he ran home to tell her mother, and was a little taken aback to be told, 'Yes, yes, dear. Now go outside and play.' A busy woman with a family of four to cope with alone, she had clearly been too preoccupied to listen properly. It was only years later, when the adult Norma discussed the incident with her, that Norma's mother realised what she had dismissed. They both knew something extraordinary had happened that day. Norma had, quite literally, sung with the voice of an angel.

★ ★ ★

Day trips can be great fun, no doubt about it. Everyone enjoys an outing to the seaside or a picnic in the country. If you've ever been on a school coach trip, you'll remember how excitement mounts as everyone climbs aboard, clutching their pack of lunchtime sandwiches – which never last beyond 10am! The suggestion of a day out is always greeted with enthusiasm, whatever your age. This certainly was the case for a group of friends in Manchester who got together every week to practise yoga. They were a pretty diverse bunch, spanning a wide range of ages, so the trip would have to accommodate a wide range of tastes and interests. North Wales, not far away from Manchester, was suggested, and somehow a trip was arranged that miraculously included something for everyone. Chatting excitedly, the group boarded the coach. 'This should be a day with a difference,' one girl remarked, little knowing just how different the trip would prove to be.

November was a little late in the year to expect good weather, but the day was dry and sunny, if a little chilly. The waterfalls were spectacular after recent heavy rain and the beaches were definitely bracing! The last stop was at a tiny old church – so tiny in fact that the interior was no bigger than the average lounge. Situated on an island and dating from the fifteenth century, it was full of atmosphere, and the surrounding countryside was stunning. Everyone was captivated.

One member of the group was a keen key board player and was very interested in the very old church organ. He had never tried to play an organ before, but he was longing to try. Eventually, encouraged by his friends, he decided to have a go. It took a little while to get the hang of it but soon he was playing the most beautiful music. The sound was wonderful and everyone was thrilled by the beautiful tone.

The tiny church was painted entirely in a soft cream colour, which reflected the light streaming through the windows. Suddenly, someone said, 'Look at the wall by the side of the organ.' All eyes focused on the spot. No one who was there that day will never forget what they saw. Slowly emerging from the wall was a figure, which, to their disbelief, appeared to be stepping out of the wall itself. The outline was clearly that of a monk, etched in a dark mushroom brown against the cream of the wall.

A woman known for her no-nonsense attitude to life objected, 'It's merely a trick of the light – the angle of the sun as it becomes low in the sky.' To test this theory several people removed their coats and placed them over the windows. The interior of the church was now fairly dark, but the figure remained as clear as before. At this point the organist stopped playing and the figure melted back into the wall, fading away gradually. Reactions at this point varied from nervous laughter to tears and bewilderment, but one fact remained irrefutable: the entire party of eighteen had witnessed an amazing sight.

For days after the trip, the main topic of conversation amongst the group was the events of that day. One of the members was convinced that the figure was in fact a guardian angel of the church; she felt it was obvious that the wonderful music had called him forth. Her husband, like many others, was incredulous and simply did not believe it. The whole incident had by now caused such a stir that the group decided they would have to pay another visit to this remarkable place.

This time, not only was their coach filled to bursting, but a convoy of cars followed on behind. A medium had been invited to join them, in the hope that she would be able to provide some sort of explanation. Everyone crowded into the little church, completely filling it. The amateur organist once more made his way to the organ, keen to play. He found to his dismay that the organ chair had been removed. He could not possibly play standing up because his feet had to pump air into the bellows on the organ. Was this an attempt to prevent the previous experience being repeated? An enterprising friend had a good idea, she would crouch beneath the organ and pump the air into it manually, enabling him to play.

For a second time, the church was filled with the most exquisite music. Everyone stood silently and waited. At last, to a collective gasp from those watching, the figure once more began to emerge from the wall. This time, however, the figure of a noble lady holding a baby also appeared. She was dressed in a high-pointed hat (known as a wimple) and was amazingly clear. She appeared to be a lady of the manor and could have been a benefactor of the church, the awe-struck observers speculated.

The medium made her way to the front of the church, where she addressed the monk. She later said that he answered her in old English, although no one else present could hear his voice. He told her he was the guardian angel of the organ. Itself a very old instrument, it had replaced one much older one when it was destroyed by fire. In his lifetime the monk had played the original organ, and he now believed it was now his duty to protect its replacement.

The fact that this amazing sequence of events was witnessed by many people in itself makes this a unique story. Several of the witnesses, as you might imagine, were so intrigued that they tried to visit the church again. This time they discovered that the resident vicar had left and the little church was locked.

Gabriel blew, and a clean, thin sound
Of perfect pitch and crystalline delicacy
Filled all the universe to the farthest star
As thin as the line separating past from future

Isaac Asimov

One person who is now completely open to the idea of angels influencing her life is Joanne. One of her favourite singers is the artist Gabrielle, with whom she feels great affinity – and it turns out that this is very apt. Life was proving very difficult for Joanne. One night when she went to bed feeling depressed and lonely, and longing for a soulmate with whom to share her life, she decided to ask God for help. This prayer triggered a chain of wonderful coincidences for Joanne, who will be eternally grateful.

The first surprising event occurred in the early hours of that night, when Joanne was woken by the sound of a song by Gabrielle. She jumped out of bed and went downstairs to find the music centre playing. It was not on a timer and appeared to have switched itself on unaided. While Joanne listened mesmerised, it played three of Gabrielle's songs. These three songs appeared to represent three stages of Joanne's life. What could this mean? she wondered. Was she being contacted by an angel?

The following weekend, her workmates encouraged her to join them in an evening out – and it was on this night that she met her soulmate. From the very moment they met there was an instant rapport. Each knew immediately that they had met their special partner.

Her interest aroused, Joanne started to read as much as she could about angels. She was amazed to discover just how often we are surrounded by these magical creatures, without even realising the fact. At this point she received from two friends an angel prayer and an angel pin, and she began to feel that her life was filled with angels.

'Coincidences' were an almost daily occurrence. A chain of them even led to a much desired new job. This job involved working with elderly patients and Joanne found herself wondering if the angels were with her in her new employment. One summer's day at work a heavy downpour suddenly appeared out of a clear blue sky. An elderly patient was walking in the grounds and, seeing the heavy rain, one of Joanne's colleagues ran to help her indoors. By the time she had ushered the old lady into the building, the young helper was soaked to the skin; the old lady, however, was completely dry! No one could quite believe their eyes. Incredulous, one of the other workers asked, 'How on earth could one person stay dry and the other be soaking wet?' Joanne answered immediately: 'The old lady was protected by the angels.' Immediately she realised that there was no doubt about it, angels were with them in this place of work. A few minutes later the staff found, under a chair, a huge, white feather. What more graphic sign did they need?

In the temples of the Far East, bells feature prominently in the worship. Indeed, in many religions bells are included at some point in the service. In Christianity bells are rung to encourage people to attend church or chapel. Peels of bells announce a wedding, and a slow mournful bell accompanies a funeral. In the Catholic mass bells are rung to mark the most important part of the service. Angels have also long been associated with bells and many accounts of angelic encounters involve their soft sounds. Sarah told me about the following experience, and how beautiful and comforting she found it to be.

Close to her sister, Julie, from childhood, Sarah was devastated to learn that seventeen-year-old Julie had a fatal illness. Indeed, the whole family was in virtual denial when the consultant told them that about a year of life was all Julie could expect. Sarah was particularly shocked, and to make matters worse she was just about to take up a job a long way from the family home. It was a dreadful twelve months for Sarah. Travelling home every weekend was exhausting and harrowing. Finally, one weekend while Sarah was at her sister's bedside along with the rest of the family, Julie peacefully died.

Arranging the funeral was a labour of love, and the family tried to include Julie's favourite poems and music. *Tubular Bells* had been a long-time favourite piece of music and so was included in the service. Picking up the pieces of everyday life after the funeral was not at all easy. Weekends felt strange for Sarah, who no longer had to dash home to her sister's side, and she missed Julie dreadfully.

Sitting alone in her flat one evening, Sarah was reading a book from a selection that had once belonged to her sister. She was finding it hard to concentrate. All at once she heard a soft ripple of bells, so soft as to be almost imperceptible. Had she imagined it? Getting up from her chair, she searched the flat for a possible explanation, but none was evident. A little later on, as she was making a hot drink in the kitchen, she heard the beautiful sound once again, but this time it was a little clearer. She wondered whether it could possibly be a contact of some kind. As she climbed into bed and turned off the light, once again she heard the music of sweet-sounding bells – this time filling the room. There was no doubt at all in her mind this time – her sister was contacting her through this lovely sound. There has not been no sound of bells since that night, but Sarah says she's got the message loud and clear – her sister is never far away.

Chapter 2

Angels of Mystery

Beside each man who's born on earth
A guardian angel takes his stand,
To guide him through life's mysteries.

Menander of Athens

A large fly buzzed lazily against the windowpane as the early spring sunshine filled the classroom with light and warmth. The class of sixteen-year-old schoolgirls looked and sounded bored, their loud sighs punctuated the shuffling of feet and pencil tapping. Their teacher, Barbara, gazed round the room in despair. What on earth could she do to arouse their interest? This was a history lesson and the GCSE exam was less than two months away. Barbara was finding the lesson quite a challenge herself, as she usually taught science and was being seconded to history for a short time. Manchester's cholera epidemic was the subject of this particular lesson, and it was failing to induce even a glimmer of interest.

At home that evening, Barbara had an idea. Getting in touch with a friend who was involved with local history, she asked if he knew of any graves belonging to cholera victims in Manchester. He said he knew such graves existed, but he was a little hazy as to their whereabouts. It's worth a try, Barbara decided. A trip out to locate them it might just create a little more interest. If the girls could read the names of the families and the ages of the children who lost their lives in the terrible epidemic, perhaps history would be brought alive for them.

A couple of days later, Barbara jumped into the school minibus and set off for the centre of the city, the girls looking cheerful and alert in the seats behind her. It seemed like a good plan to start exploring along the river bank, as it was common knowledge that this was a very old part of Manchester. It was also the site of the medieval city, which could in itself be interesting. They got off the minibus and the girls soon warmed to the adventure, trying to imagine what life would have been like so long ago. However, there was no sign of cholera graves anywhere.

Just as they were about to give up the search, several girls started to giggle and one said, 'Cor Miss, he's fit!' Turning round, Barbara saw a young man coming towards them. As severely as she could, using her best school marm voice, she said, 'Now girls, we are here to learn about history, not to stare at young men!' However, as the young man approached, she had to admit to herself that he really was very good-looking ... Barbara asked him if he knew where they might find the graveyard where Manchester's cholera victims were buried. He replied that he did and, as it was rather difficult to find, he would be pleased to take them to it.

As she walked by his side, Barbara studied the young man. He was really quite beautiful, with big blue eyes and a gentle face framed by dazzlingly blond hair. The girls had all fallen silent and were staring intently at him. He was rather strangely dressed, in a long, blue tunic and rough, almost homemade-looking boots. One pupil asked Barbara quietly if she thought he might be a gypsy and Barbara raised her finger to her lips. Nevertheless, she was wondering herself what kind of person would dress in such a way. To add to the mystery, the young man spoke in a strange manner, using the words 'thee' and 'thou'. It was all very odd, though he seemed serious enough.

Weaving its way through the small, old streets, the group eventually arrived at a high stone wall. They followed it for a short distance, until they came to a tall iron gate. The striking young man gestured to them, indicating that they should go through the gate and into a large open area of grass beyond. A steep slope led down to a flat point, where, lying neatly in rows, were many headstones. This, he announced, was the last resting place of Manchester's cholera victims.

A sense of silent awe fell over the group as they looked at the stones. The young man beckoned Barbara to see the very last gravestone in the first row. It lay against the inside of the large stone wall and appeared to be much the same as the others. Gazing into his eyes, she sensed that this was of some significance to the young man. Briefly she glanced down before immediately turning back to face him. She opened her mouth to thank him for his help, but the words froze on her lips. The young man was nowhere to be seen; in a matter of seconds he had simply disappeared! It was impossible, she thought.

Several girls screamed and asked if they had seen a ghost. Calmly, Barbara took in the facts. They stood on completely open ground; the steep slope behind them was clearly visible to them all. It would have been impossible for any one to run up that slope in seconds. Alongside the grave singled out by the young man, Barbara noticed a flight of steps leading to a large open courtyard area that was, again, in full view. It would have been impossible for him to leave swiftly in that direction, especially with his white-blond hair; he would have been seen easily. 'It was a ghost,' the girls insisted, but Barbara wasn't convinced. 'No,' she said, 'I'm certain that that was an angel.'

Well, to say that the girls were fired into action by this experience would be putting it mildly. They studied the gravestones intently and bombarded their teacher with questions. Never had a history lesson been so fascinating or exciting.

When they returned to school, Barbara told some of her colleagues about the eventful trip. One of them, intrigued by the story, grabbed her camera and said, 'Come on, let's go back and find him. This time we'll take a photo.' Off they went and searched the whole area thoroughly, making many enquires as to the whereabouts of the young man. He was after all such a distinctive-looking individual, once seen he wouldn't be easily forgotten. But all their effort was in vain. There was no trace of him to be found. Truly an angel of mystery, they concluded.

Knowing that I would be interested, Barbara told me the story and offered to take me to the graveyard to see the scene for myself. Of course, we both secretly hoped that the young angel might reappear. The graveyard was difficult to find, but at last we located it and found the grave that the young man had led Barbara to. In order to read its inscription we had to scrape away a good deal of moss from the stone, but at last it was legible. As Barbara read out the details, she suddenly gasped. There was a family in the grave: father, mother, sixteen-year-old daughter and son – approximately the age of the young man who had appeared to her and her pupils. All the girls in the school party had been sixteen – and the date of the daughter's death was actually the date of the girls' history exam in May!

Barbara was feeling a strong tingling sensation and I was reminded of details I had recently read in the Jewish sacred book, the Zohar, which talks about an 'essence' or energy belonging to a person that continues to dwell at the graveside. Sitting on a bench in the warm sunshine, we mulled over the connections while gazing at the stone. The cemetery was deserted. Deciding to go for a coffee, we passed by the grave once more. Barbara said she could feel the strong tingling sensations return when she was standing near the gravestone. She felt sure that I was meant to write down this story. It was then that we noticed, placed in the middle of the stone, a pen! Surely we could not have missed this object when standing at the graveside only moments before, and no had been near the grave; we knew that for certain. The message was all too clear: the story had to be told.

At this point, I had the distinct feeling of déjà vu. I looked around and slowly began to recognise surrounding buildings. This was an area that I had visited long ago with my grandfather. He had owned property here, although those buildings had long been demolished. I had not been in the area since I was a very young girl.

'Do you know what this place is called?' I asked Barbara.

'No,' she said.

'Angel Meadow,' I replied ...

What about the girls? Did these events have an effect on their studies? No doubt about it, their interest had been sparked by the visit, and every one passed the history exam with flying colours. One girl remarked to Barbara that she would never forget the day in the graveyard with the angel, or the cholera victims.

The name on the gravestone was Samuel Hayden. Could it have been Samuel that they saw that day? Barbara thinks so. She believes it was Samuel's intention that they should remember all that he, his family and others suffered.

★ ★ ★

'Can we please make a decision?' Jessica sighed, struggling to keep the irritation out of her voice. The six friends had been drinking coffee for what felt like hours and they still hadn't decided where they were going that evening. Time to be assertive, Jessica thought, 'Right, I'm off,' she declared. 'See you at nine in the usual bar and then we're going to a club.'

Everyone looked shocked but relieved and readily agreed. If they had difficulty making up their minds about where to go, deciding what to wear would take them the rest of the day.

As a student, Jessica found the decision easier than her friends did. Money was in short supply and her choice of clothing was pretty limited. She arrived at the bar on the dot of nine looking forward to the evening ahead. Her friends were in high spirits and they all felt sure this would surely be a night to remember.

The evening was fantastic. More and more friends joined them and they danced until the early hours of the morning. Then, suddenly the group began to feel tired. They agreed that they would all share a taxi home as usual. A large black cab was available outside and the friends piled in. The night was very cold now and a sharp frost made them shiver. The taxi driver told them this was his last fare before himself going home to a warm bed. Turning off the main road, he said, 'This way will be quicker', although by now a slight fog was forming and he had to drive more slowly than usual.

Then, without warning, a white-clad figure emerged out of the fog directly in front of the taxi. The driver slammed on his breaks and shouted an expletive. They all thought they must have run over someone. The driver jumped from the car and ran to the front, where he stared in disbelief at the empty road. There was no sign of anyone! The girls also got out of the car, checking to see if the figure was behind, underneath or at the side of the taxi. The search proved fruitless. The entire street was deserted, and yet they had all seen the figure clearly. At last the driver said, 'Come on girls, who knows what happened. Let's just get off home.'

As the taxi pulled away, Jessica felt a strange tingling sensation. She shivered. Something very strange happened tonight, she thought.

The whole incident had taken only a moment or two and they were all glad to be underway again. At this point there was a sharp bend to the left in the road. As they turned the corner the driver once again slammed on the brakes. There, directly in front of them, was a multiple car accident completely blocking the road. They could hear the sound of ambulances' sirens rushing to the scene. Once more they all climbed out of the car, but a policeman told them to get back in and go back the way they had just come.

As they settled back into the taxi once more, the girls all fell silent, but the driver spoke for all of them, 'If that person hadn't stopped us,' he said, 'we would have been right in the middle of that accident.'

Relieved to reach home at last, Jessica and her flatmate said goodnight to their friends in the taxi and went to the kitchen to make a drink. Looking Jessica in the eye, her flatmate said, 'I don't think that person was of this world.' Remembering the strange tingling sensation, Jessica could only agree. 'I think we all had a guardian angel tonight,' she replied. Her flatmate solemnly nodded.

You may be surprised to learn that fishing is the most popular sport in Britain. It never ceases to amaze me how many people like to watch others fish – it certainly doesn't have the wow factor of skating, skiing or snowboarding. For Vicky, however, fishing was an enjoyable spectator sport. She lived in the seaside town of Blackpool, where fishing was an ever-present activity. Close to her home there was a large, deep pool particularly loved by fishermen, and on warm days Vicky and her family enjoyed the atmosphere around this pool.

One day they decided to use a trip to the pool to help Vicky to get used to her new state-of-the art wheelchair – not as easy as it might sound. A strong, cheerful character who always saw the funny side of things and wanted to be as independent as possible, Vicky decided to struggle on, but in fact she hated her new chair. It was electric and very fast, with rather complicated controls. Nevertheless, she told her mother that she would be fine watching the fishermen if the rest of the family wanted to walk on a bit further. Vicky's mum, Chris, placed the wheelchair by the side of the pool and strolled off with the family for a little while. She knew that her daughter was putting on a brave face and the new chair was a source of much frustration, but she also knew that it would be overcome by Vicky's determination.

No more than a minute or two had elapsed when Chris became aware of the whirring noise of her daughter's wheelchair. Spinning around, she watched in horror as Vicky and the chair catapulted into the deep water of the pool. Rooted to the spot for an instant, Chris then screamed and ran towards the pool. All around, fishermen jumped to their feet. However, there was no sign of Vicky or the chair. Then, from nowhere it seemed, a large man appeared and dived into the pool. With the speed of lightning he was back on the surface, with Vicky held in one hand and, incredibly, the chair in the other. Even in her state of shock, Chris recalls thinking, that's impossible; he can't possibly have the strength to haul Vicky from the water with one hand and a huge heavy wheelchair with the other. However, this is exactly what happened, and the event was witnessed by dozens of people.

Gently Vicky was placed by the side of the pool. The wheelchair was then also lifted, effortlessly with one hand, onto the poolside. As Chris rushed to her daughter, the man leapt from the pool in one easy motion, landing next to Vicky. Chris looked up, saying, 'How can I ever thank you?' However, she found herself addressing a dark, wet patch on the side of the pool. The man was nowhere to be seen! There were no wet footprints leading from the wet patch and no one had seen him leave. The pool was surrounded by open grassland in all directions; it was incredible that he could simply have vanished.

Pondering on all this, Chris says an extremely tall, burly man is not most people's idea of an angel, but as far as she and Vicky are concerned, he certainly was.

For several years the Bowan family had taken their summer holiday in France. They loved the beaches, country markets and old buildings. This year, Nicola would celebrate her fifteenth birthday while on holiday and she was looking forward to doing something special. The family discovered that a not too far away from where they would be staying a huge firework display was planned on the evening of her birthday. This would be a fantastic end to her special day.

The first week of the holiday passed, the sun shining brightly the whole time, and the family spent a great deal of time on the beach. The second week however, although still very warm, was decidedly dull and overcast. On the day of Nicola's birthday she was disappointed to see a slight drizzle in the air. 'Never mind,' said her mum, 'it will be a perfect day to explore'. Getting out the map, she urged the family to look and see what they would like to do, and they decided on an area of rivers and mountains.

As they drove along, they were delighted by the number of wonderful old churches and chateaux there were to explore. Stopping at a country restaurant for lunch, they noticed that the day was considerably brighter and the mood lifted. Nicola and her brother and sister had a game of boules in the grounds of the restaurant. It was a lot of fun. They decided that they would spend the afternoon visiting a big old church in the area that the restaurant waiter had told them about. He said it contained beautiful works of art and was full of history.

They were unprepared for the sheer size of the place. It was huge, and for the moment empty of tourists save for themselves. They decanted from the car and spilled into the church, each wandering off in different directions. After exploring for some time, Nicola came across a side chapel that appeared to have been constructed entirely from marble. To the right of this chapel a wonderful staircase rose, presumably to a gallery, Nicola thought. There was something mesmerising about this flight of pure white stairs. It was filled with light and yet she could not see a window anywhere. Standing at the very bottom of the stairs she glanced upwards, aware that the light was intensifying. To her astonishment, a figure appeared at the top of the stairs seated in an alcove and surrounded by bright light. She felt the hairs on the back of her neck stand up. The figure was definitely male and wore a white suit. He did not appear to be about to move up or down the staircase; he was simply sitting still and looking directly at Nicola. Then the light began to fade and with it the strange figure. Nicola was totally perplexed, she knew it was no tourist she had just seen, and yet she felt no fear – in fact quite the opposite, she felt a sense of warmth and protection.

Turning back to the main body of the church, she looked for the rest of her family and found them assembled at the main altar. Her father smiled and said, 'Here she is. We wondered where you'd got to. Ready to leave?' Nicola nodded.

As they walked down the long aisle towards the main entrance, they passed the side chapel. 'Look at the marble staircase in here,' Nicola said, anxious to know if the rest of her family would see the man in the light. But they were perplexed and asked her what staircase she meant. To her utter disbelief, she saw that there was no staircase leading from that chapel at all. 'It was here a minute ago,' she said as her family fell about laughing. 'Right,' her brother said, 'they move marble staircases from time to time do they?' At this point Nicola decided not to say anything more about what she had seen – no one would understand, that was certain. She simply said that she had made a mistake and the staircase must have been in another part of the church.

The birthday was lovely and the firework display in the evening magnificent, but Nicola's thoughts were elsewhere. For months afterwards she wrestled with many questions. Why did it happen to her? Who was the figure? Two years later she is still not exactly sure, but she feels that this was a guardian of some description.

In times of stress, especially during exams, she has felt the same sensation she experienced in the church and a distinct feeling of the same presence. She wonders if perhaps he is here for life.

After some time had elapsed, Nicola told her mother about the incident. Far from laughing at her daughter, she said that she thought her very fortunate. 'Few people get to meet their guardian angel,' she said. We can't argue with that.

★ ★ ★

Now and then when the room was otherwise lightless
A misty grey figure would appear to be seated on this bench in the alcove.
It was the tender and melancholy figure of an angel.

Tennessee Williams

Peeping into the lounge, Samantha saw that the party was in full swing. Friends and relatives had joined her parents for a New Year's Eve celebration and clearly it was going well. 'Goodbye mum,' she said, 'see you later.' Samantha's mother gave her a kiss and told her to drive carefully. Waving a glass and shouting cheers, her father grinned his goodbye. He would not be in such a good mood, she thought, had he realised that Jason was going to drive her car. She had agreed with her boyfriend that he could drive to the party they had been invited to, and she would drive back again so he could have a drink. Samantha was not too fond of alcohol and did not mind driving home. The car had been an eighteenth birthday present from her parents, however, and her father did not like the idea of Jason driving it.

It was really only a short distance to their friend's house and they were looking forward to the party immensely. They turned into the narrow street and drove along looking for a place to park. Parking was only permitted on the side of the street where the houses were. The other side of the street was bounded by a metre-high stone wall. A steep bank fell away from the far side of the wall and dropped down to the railway line. They drove almost the whole length of the street without finding a parking place, and Jason said he would have to park in another street. No sooner had he said this than a car appeared heading in their direction and travelling at some considerable speed. There was obviously not enough room for it to pass and in a panic Jason swerved to avoid hitting it.

With a sickening thud they hit the old stone wall and demolished it, shooting through to come to a standstill at the top of the steep bank. The car seemed to fold onto Samantha and she felt a great piercing pain in her legs. Turning to Jason she saw that he was unconscious and panic rose in her throat. She wanted to scream but felt unable to make a sound. At this point she realised with horror that the car appeared to be balancing on top of the slope and could possibly hurtle down onto the railway tracks with any sudden movement. It was as if she was in a nightmare and she had no idea what would happen next. Voices could be heard approaching, and Samantha prayed it was the emergency services.

Then a soft voice said her name and a gentle hand pressed her shoulder. The relief was wonderful. She glanced into the mirror above the dashboard and saw a lady in the back seat. This must be a nurse or doctor she thought, because she was dressed in white. 'All will be well,' the voice said, 'no one will die.' Suddenly the car was surrounded by what seemed like dozens of people. As they attended to the situation, Samantha lost consciousness.

When she woke up in hospital it took Samantha a while to remember the events of the night before. It emerged that she had a broken leg, bruised ribs and a nasty whiplash injury. Jason had sustained head injuries but would be fine and was not in danger. Samantha relayed what she could remember of the accident to a policeman. 'I was so relieved to hear the lady doctor reassure me that we should be all right,' she said. The policeman looked confused. He had been first onto the scene and knew that there was no lady doctor in the car. 'Are you sure there was a lady doctor there, dear?' he asked.

'Yes,' said Samantha, 'she had her white coat on.'

'But the ambulance had an all-male crew that night,' he told her, 'and none of them had a white uniform. The mind can play odd tricks in this kind of situation,' he continued. 'You mustn't worry'.

Knowing instinctively that this was a time to keep quiet, Samantha smiled. She realised with a wonderful warm glow exactly what the lady in white on the back seat of her car was. 'Thank you, angel,' she said softly to herself.

* * *

By the time she celebrated her sixteenth birthday, it was clear that Lisa would have to re-think her career plan. Cutting her birthday cake she said, laughing, 'It's obvious to me that I can't be a fairy' – an idea she had announced as a child.

'Somehow, at 5ft 10, I think you blew your chances by growing,' said her mum.

'To be serious, though', Lisa replied, 'I have decided to stay on at school, take my A levels and then do a degree in nursing.'

The entire family was delighted by this news and agreed that she was sure to be very successful.

Lisa's career plan got off to a good start. She passed her A levels and accepted a place at university to study for a degree in nursing. Her ambition had not wavered for a moment; indeed, she was keener than ever to get started at university. Her room in halls turned out to be very pleasant and soon looked cosy with pictures and ornaments from home. Lisa met some of the other girls for a cup of coffee in the communal kitchen, and she felt that she would make some good friendships. In short, she was very happy and convinced that she wanted a role in life where she could help people.

On the morning of her first lecture Lisa woke at the crack of dawn. Wide awake with excitement, she knew that there was no chance of going back to sleep. Pulling on her dressing gown, she tiptoed down the corridor to the kitchen. She thought a couple of slices of toast might calm her down. Placing the bread in the toaster, she was aware of a slight noise behind her. Spinning round she saw a woman standing in the open doorway. She was wearing a dark blue ground-length dress, a starched white apron and a cap with ties under the chin. She glanced briefly at Lisa then turned and walked down the corridor. What a strange woman, thought Lisa, and how odd that uniform was. Perhaps the staff are dressing up just for today, she mused. Maybe it's a way of greeting the new students and illustrating history.

It was a long but exciting day, and Lisa was glad to be back in her own room eventually, relaxing and taking stock of events. By now she was very tired – after all, she had been up very early that morning. One thing is for sure, Lisa thought, I have made exactly the right choice of career. Looking at the mountain of books on her desk, however, she knew that it would entail a lot of hard work. As she lifted one large, heavy book from the top of the pile, she accidentally dropped it. It fell open with a thud. Lisa bent to pick it up and let out a gasp. The book had fallen open at a page containing a large photograph of a woman. It was without a doubt the same woman she had seen that morning in the kitchen doorway. The caption underneath the photograph said 'Florence Nightingale'!

I should like to add a little postscript to this story. I was told some time ago that Florence Nightingale was buried in the grounds of the Unitarian chapel at East Wellow, near Romsey in Hampshire. One Sunday a lady was visiting this chapel and, finding herself a little early for the service, went inside and sat quietly in a pew. Presently a woman walked down the aisle and into the vestry. She was strangely dressed and the visitor thought her rather odd. Eventually other people arrived for the service and the worship got underway. Chatting to the minister after the service, the lady told him that she had arrived early, and he apologised for leaving her alone in the chapel to wait. 'There was one other person here,' she said and described the odd-looking woman.

'Come with me,' said the minister, leading her into the vestry. Inside, there was a picture hanging on the wall in a prominent position. 'Was that the lady you saw?' he asked.

'Why, yes,' she said, leaning forward to read the caption underneath. To her astonishment, it read 'Florence Nightingale'!

It emerged that this was not the first time visitors and members of the congregation had seen her. Indeed, other than visitors, few people are surprised any more by a sighting of Florence Nightingale.

★ ★ ★

Toby was thrilled to receive an invitation to his friend Rob's eighteenth birthday bash. His mother was decidedly less enthusiastic. Toby had only been driving a short time and to get to the party he would have to drive across the Pennines ... in winter. Anyone who knows the Pennines will tell you just how high the road is and how quickly the weather can change. Toby had virtually no experience of motorway driving, and the whole idea filled his mother with terror. Nothing would deter Toby, however, and on the day of the party he was in high spirits as he said goodbye to his parents. The weather was bitter cold and pretty frosty. If only it was May instead of February, his mother thought.

The party was excellent and Toby thoroughly enjoyed himself. In the early hours of the morning he said goodbye to his friends and left for home. Normally he would have stayed the night, but he had to play in a football match the following morning and did not want to miss it. As he made his way towards the motorway, he was aware of snow gently falling and it made him feel a little uneasy. I have never driven in snow, he thought. I hope it doesn't get any heavier. This was not to be, however. As he approached the slipway to the motorway, the snow was falling quite thickly and looked as if it was going to last. There was very little traffic at that time of the morning, but what there was had soon slowed to a crawl. The windscreen wipers were barely coping with the snow and Toby was very uneasy indeed. After what seemed like a lifetime, he realised that he was in fact only about half way across the Pennines, and his heart sank at the thought of the long way he had yet to drive.

Suddenly his heart lifted as a very familiar sight came into view. It was the white and bright blue van that belonged to a neighbour.

Flashing his lights as he passed Toby, the driver slowed down, enabling Toby to follow behind. What a comfort it was to tuck in behind the familiar van, safe in the knowledge that he had a friend close by. Eventually they reached the close where they both lived. Toby thankfully turned into his drive. His neighbour waved and flashed his lights before driving further along the close to his own house. Collapsing into bed Toby fell into a deep sleep.

Morning came all too soon, however, and he had to leave the warmth and comfort of his bed to go to football. His mother, overjoyed to see him safe and sound, was making him breakfast. Toby told her of the events of the night before and how relieved he had been to see the neighbour in his van. Toby's mum and dad exchanged nervous glances. 'Are you sure it was him?' Toby's mum asked.

'Yes of course,' he answered – after all, their neighbour had his name emblazoned on the side of his van in huge letters. Then, gathering his kit, Toby went to play football.

After he had gone, his mum walked down the close. It was as she thought: there was the van, snow piled up against the tires and no sign of tracks. According to the neighbour's wife it had not moved for three days, since her husband had died of a heart attack.

What angel nightly tracks that waste of frozen snow?

Emily Brontë

★ ★ ★

The following story was told to me by an acquaintance who lives in the Lake District. It was to become a real mystery and was reported in the local paper by a very surprised journalist.

A cottage caught fire in a small village, and the flames swiftly became fierce. It was impossible for anyone to enter the building, though several tried. Neighbours watched in horror, as the flames grew higher, praying that the fire brigade would arrive as soon as possible. Then it emerged that a baby was trapped in an upstairs bedroom alone. This greatly added to the distress of the onlookers, who shouted the information to the approaching firemen. Just then, the figure of a young woman appeared at the bedroom window, holding the baby in her arms. There was a gasp from the crowd as she opened the window and threw the baby to the safety of the arms of a waiting fireman.

The crowd's relief at the baby's rescue turned to despair as the young woman was engulfed in the flames, surely to perish. No one knew her. There had been no one except the family in the cottage that night and all were now accounted for. Eventually the firemen brought the blaze under control and were able to enter the cottage. They searched every room for the young girl but there was no trace of her. There was not a body in any of the rooms nor any evidence pointing to the fact that she had been in the bedroom and rescued the baby. It was truly baffling.

One onlooker, however, finally plucked up courage to tell the police that he had in fact recognised the young girl. She was a girl who had lived in the area many years ago. One day she had simply disappeared and was, after much searching and many investigations, presumed to be dead. On hearing this, the newspaper called her the 'fire angel'. Few would disagree.

I settled thankfully into my seat aboard the London to Manchester train. It had been a very hot day and now the early evening was not showing any signs of cooling down. The train was almost full and there were just a few minutes to wait before we pulled out of Euston. Suddenly, a small, frail-looking girl carrying a huge suitcase came panting into the train. Pushing her suitcase into the luggage area at the carriage entrance, she stared at her ticket in confusion. 'Could you please tell me where this seat is?' she asked me in halting English. Glancing at the ticket, I assured her that it was the one directly opposite mine. With a shy 'thank you' and a sigh of relief, she too sank into her seat.

The train departed. The girl began to relax and, after a cold drink, she started to chat to me. She said she had arrived in London from Brazil earlier in the day and was on her way to stay with friends in Manchester, who had bought her ticket and sent it to her. At the airport she had been put on a coach that she thought would drop her at Euston. Instead, it took her into the centre of London and dropped her somewhere – she had no idea where – in the middle of the huge bustling city. Trying not to panic, she hailed a taxi and asked if it would take her to Euston Station. The only problem was that she had no English currency, no idea how or where she might change a traveller's cheque and very little time to reach the train she was booked on.

She struggled to communicate in English, trying to urge the importance of her journey on the taxi driver. However, the more anxious she became, the less sense she made, and the taxi driver simply shrugged his shoulders. In despair she covered her face with her hands. Gently a much larger hand removed them from her face. 'What is the problem?' a tall, English gentleman asked. As clearly as she was able, she told her story. Leaning into the cab, he asked the driver how much the fare was to Euston. Then, taking the money from his pocket, he handed the taxi driver the fare plus some extra to ensure that he showed the girl to her train at Euston, and off sped the taxi.

'What a nightmare!' she said. The strangest thing of all, however, was that on gratefully climbing into the taxi, she had leant through the open window to thank the man profusely for his kindness, only to find no one there. The pavement was empty. She looked through the windows behind her and in front, but he was nowhere to be seen. 'He was so tall,' she said, 'with blond hair. How on earth could he have disappeared in only seconds?' I smiled – of all the people on the train she was asking me, the author of books about angels!

Before I could answer, the lady sitting next to me, who had been nodding all the way through this account, piped up: 'It was your guardian angel, dear.' 'Absolutely,' said the girl from Brazil, 'and what perfect timing.'

The equation of appearance and disappearance, the truth
of the body and the nobody,
The vision of the presence that dissolves into splendour:
pure vitality, a heartbeat of time.

Octavio Pax

Our next story also involves a train journey, this time from the south of England to Scotland.

The train was approaching the city of Glasgow, and Sophia decided that the butterflies in her tummy had turned into large bats. She was so nervous her hands shook as she read the train time table once more. How she hated having to change trains. She had had to do it twice already on this long journey, and now not only did she have to change trains but also stations. Perhaps there's a bus connecting the stations she thought, but she was anxious because she knew she didn't have much time to catch her next train.

For the first time, she thought her mother had been right all along, at sixteen she was too young to leave home. She gazed at the glossy brochure once more to reassure herself. It contained a photograph of the most beautiful-looking hotel, set in acres of rolling countryside. The staff quarters appeared very smart and spacious, and the tartan uniform was actually rather attractive. It will all be fine, she thought. I'll make new friends and learn a lot about the hotel trade. She was, however, far from convinced as she stepped from the train and felt the colour drain from her face.

Outside the bustling station, she gazed around for someone to ask directions to the other city station. Aware suddenly of someone at her left shoulder, she turned round to see a very tall man smiling down at her. She felt a sudden sense of peace and confidence.'Here we are,' he said, lifting her suitcase onto the bus stationed at the curb. Climbing on behind, her continued,' Don't worry, I'm here to help.'

A short time later the bus pulled up outside the station and the passengers got off. Once more the tall man took Sophia's bag and directed her to follow him. Strangely, he did not appear to have any luggage himself, not even a briefcase, but Sophia was so relieved to have help that she obediently trotted along behind him. He strode purposefully onto a platform and indicated to Sophia that she should climb aboard the waiting train. Gladly she jumped on the train and the man followed. He placed her suitcase on the rack above her head and then sat down opposite her, taking a book from his pocket and settling down to read. Within a few moments the train was pulling away and Sophia relaxed, knowing that finally she was on the last leg of a very long journey.

It must have been an hour and a half or so later that Sophia took the letter from her handbag containing the details of where to get off the train and who would meet her. Startled to see the tall man putting away his book and getting to his feet, she instinctively pulled on her coat. 'Here we are,' he told her, taking her suitcase from the rack and moving to the train door. The little country station where the train came to a halt was surrounded by green fields. In the small car park, however, Sophia could see a man standing beside a Range Rover, obviously waiting for a passenger. Making her way towards him, the tall man still carrying her suitcase, she waved and was relieved to hear him shout, 'Sophia ?'

'Yes,' she replied and at once felt her spirits rise – he had such a warm, friendly face. The tall man placed Sophia's suitcase down as she shook hands with the hotel manager. Quickly remembering her manners, she turned to say thank you, but now there was no sign of him – not in the car park nor on the open station, and the train had already left. He could not possibly have made it back to the train in those few seconds. How very mysterious, she thought, but was soon caught up in the journey to the hotel and the tour she was given on arrival.

Alone in her beautiful room later that night, she collected her thoughts for the first time that day. All at once she was stunned by the mysterious help she had received. When she arrived outside Glasgow station, how did the tall man know she was going to another station? She had not told him; he had simply shepherded her onto the bus. Stranger still, he had guided her to the exact train she needed but, she hadn't told him where she was travelling to. How could he have possibly known? Finally, she had not told him where she needed to leave the train – indeed she herself hadn't a clue in her state of fright – and yet he had made sure she got off the train at the right station. The uncanny way he had disappeared completed the feeling that something very unusual indeed had occurred.

When I met Sophia, I asked her if she could describe the man accurately.

'He was well over six feet in height,' she answered. 'His hair was almost white-blonde and his eyes were a deep blue. He was difficult to miss even in a crowd, never mind a deserted car park.' Then she asked me, 'Do you really think he was an angel?'

'Well,' I concluded, 'there are only two possible explanations: either there is a very tall blond man, circumnavigating Britain's railways in search of damsels in distress, or he was an angel with special responsibility for railways!'

★ ★ ★

It was a beautiful day in July and the little shop was busy with customers. It was Wednesday, market day in this Lancashire town, and the market always bought customers into the shop in droves. The staff took turns to take their breaks on market days.

After a morning selling books, toys and stationery, Barbara was very hungry as she climbed the stairs to the first floor. Store rooms, staff rooms and a kitchen were situated on this floor, and at the very end of the corridor there was a boiler room. There was also an alcove in the corridor where the staff could safely leave personal belongings. Barbara took her handbag from the alcove before going into the kitchen to eat lunch. Her colleague, Elaine, was just finishing her lunch break and shouted 'hello' to Barbara.

As she turned from the alcove and looked up, Barbara saw a young man push through a set of fire doors and then through the door leading into the boiler room. This was decidedly odd. No one had followed Barbara up the stairs and she had not heard any footsteps. The young man was smartly dressed in a T-shirt, black trousers and shoes, not the type of clothes worn by someone working on a boiler. 'Elaine,' Barbara asked, 'who's the young man going into the boiler room?' Her friend had no idea and had not in fact seen anyone.

Together they walked through the two fire doors and into the boiler room – rather gingerly but feeling there was safety in numbers. Opening the door, they found the room, as usual, in complete blackness. It had no windows and the light had to be switched before they could see anything at all. The light switch could only be reached by stepping a little way into the room. Barbara quickly located the switch and turned on the light. There was no one in the room except the two of them.

The two girls went downstairs to ask if anyone had given a young man permission to enter the first-floor area. They were told that no one had been through the shop door leading to the stairs except for themselves. The service desk was at the back of the shop, and you had to pass behind it in order to reach the staircase – impossible without being seen. In any case, the boiler was in perfect working order, and no one had ordered any repairs.

'Right,' said Barbara, 'let's recap: no one followed me up the stairs and I heard no footsteps. Elaine did not see or hear anyone while she was in the kitchen, despite the door being open, and the man I saw would have had to walk past the kitchen. But he went into the boiler room – I saw him clearly. He didn't leave the room, but when we went in, the room was empty!' There simply was no explanation, they all agreed. It was very odd.

In the end, they all decided that the figure Barbara had seen had to be supernatural. 'Do you suppose he was trying to tell us something?' she asked her colleagues. 'Is there a message we haven't picked up?'

The following week Barbara was at home on her day off, when the phone rang. It was a colleague from the shop. There was dreadful news. Out of the blue they had received a fax telling them that the business was in trouble and the shop was going to close, with the loss of all their jobs. And, indeed, only days later the shop was closed for the last time. The staff were sad and shocked. 'One thing is clear, though,' Barbara said, 'the mysterious man was obviously there to warn us. Angels often appear in everyday clothing. He was trying to prepare us for the worst – and perhaps to reassure us that eventually all will be well.'

During the process of writing this book, I was privileged to receive a letter of congratulation from Dr. H Moolenburgh. Long before I started to research the angel phenomenon, I read Dr. Moolenburgh's book *A Handbook of Angels*. A Dutch GP, he had listened to his patients talk of angel experiences and began to research the subject. His work inspired and fascinated me, and I was thrilled to discover that my books, recently translated into Dutch, shared the same publisher as Dr. Moolenburgh's.

Something that Dr. Moolenburgh and I have in common is the failure to recognise angel intervention in our own lives until much later. So often I have listened to accounts or angelic encounters, only to realise that I have had the same experience. The story that Dr. Moolenburgh gave me to share with you illustrates how this has happened in his life too.

Some years ago Dr. Moolenburgh and his wife were returning to Holland from the South of France. They planned to drive their car onto the train at Avignon and travel home in comfort. Having 200 km to drive before reaching the train station and lots of time, they decided to have a picnic on the way. Late in the morning, a little before lunch time, they found themselves driving down a long, lonely stretch of country road. It was beautiful and isolated and would make a good place to stop and picnic.

The sides of the road were rather overgrown with long grass. As Dr. Moolenburgh reversed his car to park along this edge, he was suddenly aware of a bump. When he went to investigate he discovered that hidden in the long grass was a short concrete pole, on which he had speared the car. It was now absolutely stuck. The couple's hearts sank. How on earth would they ever reach the train? No car had passed on this lonely road and, try as they might, it was impossible to release the car from the pole.

Suddenly a lady on a bicycle rode into sight. Dr. Moolenburgh thought that maybe help was now at hand, but she simply added to the gloom by telling him that even if there had been a garage near, as it was Sunday, it would be shut. There was, she said, a convent not too far away, but the nuns would not be of any help. Smiling cheerfully, she rode away, leaving them in deep despair.

Suddenly brightening, Mrs Moolenburgh said, 'Don't lose hope. Help will come.'

At that very moment, two red cars – the first they had seen in a long time – came around the bend towards them. The cars stopped and one of the drivers asked, 'Need help?' He and his wife got out of their car, as did the couple in the second car. The Moolenburghs noticed that the cars had English registration plates, the only English plates they had seen on their holiday. Without much more ado, the four travellers took hold of the bumper of Dr. Moolenburgh's car. One of them shouted 'one, two, three' and together they lifted the car clean away from the concrete pole. As the four travellers went back to their cars, the man who had first offered help turned slowly to the Moolenburghs and gave them a slow knowing smile – as if almost mocking their astonishment at events. Then, without another word being spoken, the four drove away.

Jumping into their freed car as quickly as possible, the Moolenburghs swiftly set off, anxious now to catch the train, all thoughts of a picnic gone. Despite the fact that only minutes had elapsed since the four travellers had departed, nowhere on that lonely stretch of road did they see the two red cars. Where could they have got to? It was as if they had vanished into thin air.

Later, at home, Dr. Moolenburgh wrote in his diary, 'It was just like a story from my angel book.' As time passed, the enigmatic smile of the man remained as clear as crystal in his mind and eventually the truth dawned on him. No wonder the smile had been slightly mocking – as if to say, 'You of all people should recognise what is happening here.' How often had he written about people being helped by angels in everyday clothing who suddenly disappear? Finally he realised that these normal-looking tourists, were actually nothing of the kind!

Chapter 3

Fur, Feathers and Rockets!

Sacred or secular, what is the difference?
If every atom inside our bodies was once a star
Then all is sacred and secular at the same time.

Gretel Ehrlich

I think you will agree that there is something quite magical about stars. Not only are they incredibly beautiful but we feel that they are linked with our destiny. Few can resist reading their stars in magazines and newspapers. Early mariners relied exclusively on the stars for guidance, and the great pyramids of Egypt were built using the stars as a template. From ancient times, mankind has been fascinated by the night sky and the symbolism of stars. The Magi, or three wise men, were very astute astronomers; indeed, it is from the word *magi* that we get the modern word 'magic'. These clever men were highly respected, capable of reading warnings and predicting the future from the stars. They were followers of Zoroastra, a man who founded a religion in 500 BC. He was the first person to record having seen an angel, and angels featured prominently in this new religion. Some ancient peoples believed that the stars were angels, insisting that you must never point to a star because you would offend the angels. Looking at the stars and asking for help could be the origin of the expression 'wish upon a star'.

Joan and her family certainly feel an affinity with the stars. This is their story.

'We're going to live in Fiji,' John told his mother. He knew that this announcement would provoke mixed emotions. His mother was, of course, happy for him, but she was sad that her son and his wife, along with her lovely little granddaughter, would be living so far away. Soon all the arrangements were complete, the house was sold and everyone was preparing for departure. It was an exciting time for all, especially Martha, Joan's granddaughter. For her, this was a huge adventure.

While all this was happening, I was visiting New York. I had been invited to speak about angels and had taken the opportunity to meet up with a friend to tour the sights. We had had a great time and were tired when we boarded the night flight back to England. Delighted to find the plane sparsely populated, we stretched out, preparing for a comfortable flight.

At one point the pilot announced that if we looked out of the windows, we would have an excellent view of Hale bop, the comet. Sure enough, there it was, magnificent against the night sky. At 30,000 feet there was not a trace of light pollution to spoil the view. Indeed, the view of all the stars was breathtaking. I was carried away by this sight, and therefore decidedly taken aback when my friend suddenly asked, 'Would you like a cat?' Perplexed, to say the least, I asked her why. Well it appeared that this little cat was called Daisy and belonged to Martha – the same Martha who was about to leave for Fiji. Try though they might, the family had been unable to find a home for Daisy and this was causing much distress to all involved. Martha's grandmother, Joan, was especially upset by this predicament. She could not look after Daisy herself because she was allergic to cats, and everyone else had either refused point blank or already had animals to look after. What on earth were they going to do?

When I got home I asked my family if we could give a home to Daisy. The answer was yes, and Martha, her mother and her grandmother all arrived with the very beautiful tabby in a basket, crying pitifully. It was a happy ending, even though Daisy did not immediately appreciate this fact. Martha's grandmother told me how grateful and relieved they were. Finding a home for Daisy had seemed like the last straw and had heightened the emotions of everyone involved. It turned out that the night we were flying back from New York, she had had friends to dinner and had told them of her worries about Daisy. 'Look to the stars,' said one of her visitors. 'You will find the answer.' Of course, she was flabbergasted when I told her I had been asked to take Daisy while looking at the stars.

As I write this story, Daisy is sitting on the computer desk, bolt upright. As I tell her this story, she listens intently. 'Do you have an angel sitting on a star?' I ask her. I swear she winked at me.

I have another story featuring a cat, but this one does not have a happy ending. It's a mysterious and symbolic story, and very moving. You may remember Andrew from Chapter 1. A talented musician, this lively young man died in his late teens, devastating his entire family and large circle of friends. The family owned a large black cat which was never far from Andrew's side.

The day before Andrew's funeral a close family friend went to arrange the flowers in the church. This labour of love would take most of the day, as she wanted to make a beautiful floral tribute to Andrew. As she entered the church she was amazed to see a large black cat follow her inside. To her knowledge (and she was a church member) there had never been a cat in church before. The cat sat quietly all day, intently watching her arrange the flowers. When she had finished, it slowly stood up and left the church with her. She made enquiries, but no one had any knowledge of a black cat, either in the church or in the surrounding area. It did not belong to anybody in the nearby houses. It was a complete mystery where it had come from. To add to this mystery, no one has seen the cat since that day.

I was thinking about this cat when I happened upon a book about ancient Egypt. I knew that the Egyptians worshipped cats and that cats actually lived in the temples. The Egyptian cat goddess was called Bast. She was depicted with the head of a cat and she was associated with music – yet another link with Andrew.

Teacher says every time a bell rings,
an angel gets his wings.

Karolyn Grimes

I think most teachers would tell you that the classroom has more little devils than angels. However, for one teacher at least, angels were present.

Beverley teaches in a large comprehensive school and describes her job as 'challenging'. In order to be one step ahead of all the work involved in a school day, Beverley was in the habit of arriving at school very early every morning. The calm before the storm of the pupils arriving provided a much needed period of quiet preparation. Many mornings she wished that the day could stay so calm.

Arriving at school one morning at 7am, Beverley settled at her desk as usual. Before starting her preparation, she took from her handbag the book she had been reading about angels. She found it soothing and inspiring and she began to read it aloud. Then she asked the angels to be with her and to sustain the calm throughout the day. Closing the book, she gazed around her at the empty classroom, soaking up the stillness. Her attention was drawn to the window. Suddenly, to her astonishment, a large, white feather drifted gently past the window out of a clear blue sky. So slowly did it drift to the ground that for a moment Beverley could only gaze in wonder.

Then she realised that she had been contacted by angels and that this was a sign of their presence. It truly was, she says, a moment to treasure. Confidence and strength to face the coming day flooded through her and she awaited the arrival of the pupils with a sense of deep calm. It was a notably different day. Her pupils behaved with a quiet diligence she had never seen before. At the end of the day, one of Beverley's colleagues remarked in amazement how calm and peaceful the entire school had been that day. Beverley smiled and silently thanked the angels.

Shortly after receiving Beverley's story another account of angels making their presence felt in school reached me. Perhaps there are more angels in the classroom than we imagine. But this story comes from a very different school from the previous one – a tiny village junior school set amongst beautiful scenery in Scotland. Janet was struggling with a real problem in this usually pleasant school. One of her pupils was being bullied. The boy in question had not complained but the evidence was plain to see. She tried talking to the class, reasoning with them, hoping to appeal to their better nature. It was all to no avail. The boys she strongly suspected of causing all the problems hotly denied it, leaving Janet feeling helpless and at a loss as to what to do next. It was a relief when the Christmas holidays came around and the school closed for two weeks. Maybe the season of good will will rub off on the bullies, she thought, but without much hope in her heart.

January brought a very cold start to the year and on the first day of term it started to snow heavily. Stepping outside her front door, Janet thought how magical it looked. As she glanced up at a tree in her garden covered with snow, the thought went through her head that the branches reminded her of angel wings. As if from nowhere, a prayer formed in her mind: 'Please, God, let your angels to help me today.' Not generally a religious person by any means, Janet was surprised at herself.

Morning assembly was a cheerful affair, the pupils excited by the snowfall and looking forward to morning break, when they could have some fun outside. The atmosphere was light and pleasant as Janet started the first lesson of the day. A boy suddenly called to her, 'Miss, the snow is coming in through the window.' Turning, she saw what appeared to be large flakes of snow beneath the windowsill at the far end of the room. Leaving her desk, she walked across the room to investigate. She drew in her breath sharply on approaching the window – for what had appeared to be snow was in fact a pile of soft, white feathers! Turning to the class with a broad smile on her face, Janet said, 'Nothing to worry about; everything will be fine.' And from that day on, she says, everything was: the bullying stopped and the class began to get on well together.

One more story of feathers, though not in a school this time. These feathers appeared in a very unusual and very dramatic way. Alison felt very close to the angels and often asked for their help. Then circumstances arose in which she needed the angels more than ever ...

Alison and her mother lived in the north of England. Her mother had become very worried about her own step-mother, who lived alone many miles away in Newmarket. Although she wasn't very emotionally attached to her step-mother, nevertheless she felt a great sense of responsibility for her. Eventually, the step-mother died. Full of apprehension, Alison's mother made the long drive to Newmarket to arrange the funeral and undertake the problematical task of sorting out the house and its contents. Alison was worried about her and felt that the best thing she could do to help was ask the angels to be with her mother at this difficult time.

Ten days passed and the funeral took place to everyone's satisfaction. But the worst task of all still lay ahead. The furniture and personal belongings had to be dealt with. It was hard physical work, which also involved a great deal of cleaning. At the beginning of this task, Alison's mother decided to take off her wedding and engagement rings for safety so they wouldn't get damaged while she worked. She put them in her purse and put the purse in her handbag. Meanwhile, knowing how stressful the situation would be for her mother, Alison meditated on the angels many times each day, asking them for their help.

At last the job was finished, the furniture and belongings dealt with and the house spotless. Sighing with relief, Alison's mother rang her daughter before setting out for home. 'All finished,' she said. 'I'm just about to drive home'. Alison told her to take care, adding that she felt sure the angels would be accompanying her, as she had asked them to be with her mother the whole time. 'Thank you,' her mother said. 'See you soon.'

It was a lovely feeling starting the car and setting off for home again. But having driven for only a few hundred yards, Alison's mum was suddenly gripped with panic, for she noticed that her rings were missing. She stopped the car, her heart pounding, and collected her thoughts. Then she remembered that she had put the rings in her purse for safety. She quickly pulled the purse from her handbag and opened it, to find the rings safe and sound. Scarcely able to believe her eyes, however, she saw nestling with the rings a soft, white, feather! It seemed impossible. She hadn't touched her purse since she put the rings in. Trembling, she rang her daughter again and told her with excitement that the angels really had looked after her, and, what's more, they had left a calling card. Alison laughed with delight, 'I knew they would, Mum,' she said. 'See you soon and take care.' Her heart told her that the angels would be with her mother all the way home.

When we think of signs and symbols of angels, feathers, birds or even flowers probably come to mind, but perhaps not rockets. But for Helen rockets – and in this case the kind of rocket I'm referring to is a firework – were an inspirational message from the next world. Her story is unique and reassuring.

Helen had a kind and supportive partner in Bill. He helped her to cope with the death of her mother, a very distressing event for Helen. She had no faith in life after death and the finality of death, as she saw it, was difficult to bear. However, Bill had a very strong belief in the after-life. He would gently try to persuade Helen to consider the possibility that something more did exist, knowing that the belief could bring her great comfort.

But soon after her mother's death, there was more terrible news for Helen. As a child Bill had suffered from cancer; now, sadly, the cancer had returned, and this time there was no hope of a cure. The distress Helen felt, so soon after the loss of her mum, was immeasurable. Life without Bill was unthinkable and she had no idea how she would cope. Bill, though, was as strong as ever; his belief did not waver and he assured Helen that he was not in the least afraid to die. 'I will simply move on to another life,' he told her. How Helen wished she could believe him.

In November 2001 Bill died and Helen felt her world crumble. Her loneliness was compounded by the fact she lived in a very remote part of the Scottish Highlands. The scenery was wonderful, but her home was so isolated and the terrain so difficult, that friends had to leave their cars a mile or so from the house and walk.

Following Bill's wishes, the date of the funeral was November the 5th – he wanted a day of fireworks and joy for his service. Friends suggested that after the funeral they should let off rockets to celebrate Bill's life. That evening everyone gathered in the garden behind Helen's house and watched the rockets soar into the night sky. The symbolism was perfect. The exploding stars brought colour to the sky, reflecting not only Bill's personality but also the fact that he was now happy in heaven. A family friend had found five very unusual rockets to send heavenwards in Bill's memory. No one had ever seen rockets like this before. They were large and unusual in shape and colour. They all assumed that they had been imported. The only hitch in the celebration was the fact that the last rocket failed to ignite. Helen gently lifted it out of the earth and placed it on a patch of waste ground where it wouldn't be a danger to the children present.

As Helen was so isolated, it was decided that her sister would stay with her for a while. Although, owning no less than eleven bull mastiff dogs, Helen felt very secure, she was very happy to have some company for a while. She was even more grateful when solicitor's letters arrived with very depressing news concerning Bill's estate. Helen was at her lowest ebb for years.

One morning, pondering on the depressing sequence of events, she opened the front door and, to her amazement, found placed squarely on her doorstep ... a rocket! It was exactly the same unusual type of rocket they had bought for Bill's funeral. Helen was puzzled. Firstly, these rockets were not readily available in Scotland; secondly no one ever 'just passed' the house; thirdly, the dogs had not barked; and fourthly Bill's car was still parked in the drive, obscuring the view of the house. No one could simply have thrown the rocket and have it land accurately on the step. What a mystery! Calling for her sister to confirm that the incident wasn't just a trick of her imagination, Helen went to the patch of waste ground and retrieved the rocket that had failed to ignite. The women compared the two fireworks. No doubt about it, they were identical.

Bemused, they went to the kitchen for a cup of tea. Could this be a sign from Bill? Helen wondered. Three or four of the dogs lay by the fire and all was peaceful as the sisters sipped their tea. Suddenly, they heard Bill's voice loud and clear saying, 'Helen.' Even the dogs jumped to their feet and stared transfixed in the direction of the voice. There was no doubt now in Helen's mind; this surely was a message of support.

There was to be further communication from Bill. His car had to be taken away, and this, of course, was another distressing event for Helen to cope with. When the car was moved, there on the floor by the front passenger seat was another rocket, again identical to the others. Not being able to drive, Helen had always sat in this seat. Helen placed this new rocket by the front doorstep alongside the others, and it felt as if they were somehow protecting Helen and her house.

It was by now mid-January and the middle of a very bad winter. Heavy snow and frost brought all sorts of difficulties, including frozen pipes and faulty heating – problematic in this remote spot. Helen completely forgot about the rockets lying under the deep snow. At long last spring arrived. Slowly the snow began to melt and the rockets emerged, still in line, by the front doorstep. Scarcely able to believe her eyes, Helen noticed that the rockets were completely intact. Impossible, she thought, but after months beneath wet snow the colours on the casings had not faded and the rockets appeared exactly as they had months before. Rushing indoors, Helen grabbed her camera and took photographs of the amazing rockets.

It would be wonderful to report that this was the end of Helen's problems, but, sadly, this was to prove the most difficult year of her life. A bad fall resulted in broken ribs and a chest infection. Helen lay in bed wondering when her luck would change. Sitting up in bed gingerly one Sunday morning and feeling very sorry for herself, for the first time in her life she started to pray. She asked God for his help, asking that he might send his angels. Some time later she struggled to get out of bed and was astonished to see on the carpet a huge, white feather. The bedroom windows and door had been firmly closed all night. Feelings of peace and love flooded through her – her prayer had been answered. Again she found her camera and photographed the feather where it lay.

For Helen this was a sign that she was not alone. At the points in her life where she seemed beyond help, symbols had appeared to comfort her. Faith had been restored to Helen. She now has no doubt that an after-life awaits us. Just when you think you can go no further, take one more step, turn one more corner – you never know, your angel may be waiting around that corner.

Of all the signs and symbols people attribute to angelic presence, the most commonly occurring must be the white feather. Many ancient peoples believed that they were linked to heaven by feathers. Native Americans wore a feathered head dress not to make them look fierce in war, as people commonly believe, but to connect them to the spirit in the sky. I receive letters from all over the world telling me that feathers appear when people expect them least, and usually when they need reassurance most. I would like at this point to tell you about my own experience of finding a white feather.

My local bookshop, Sweetens, in Bolton, Lancashire, is a very special place. It's a haven for shoppers, and the manager supports local authors whenever possible. In 2002 my book *Saved by the Angels* was published, and Stella, the shop's own angel, arranged a launch party for me. It was a wonderful day. Crowds of people came to buy the book, forming a long queue to get their copy signed. Many of these people were anxious to tell me about their own angelic experiences, and I was astonished at how many involved finding a white feather.

Eventually the book-signing came to an end and I prepared to join friends and family for a buffet in a reception room above the shop. As I stood up, a friend of mine suddenly stared at the floor. 'Look under the chair,' she said. There underneath the chair was a large, white, feather. It did seem particularly appropriate on that special day. I left the feather in the shop to encourage the angels to stay there.

Thanks to the publicity given to the event that day, Sweetens sold many books and had to order more from the publisher. A box of my books duly arrived and was opened by Debbie one of the shop assistants. She was unprepared for what she found. On top of the box of books was a layer of white feathers! Bookshops, of course, receive boxes of books on a daily basis but this was the first time one had ever arrived topped with feathers. I think we can safely assume that the angels are at home in Sweeten's bookshop.

Chapter 4

Angelic Encounters Worldwide

Angels need no passport.

Cary Grant

Angels certainly don't need permission of any description to visit anywhere in the world. They move between every country, transcending religion and gender, to help mortals everywhere. They have even been seen in space, as several astronauts will testify. Stories reach me constantly from all corners of the globe. This chapter contains just a few of them.

I love the American expression 'fall'. It's so very evocative and describes the season perfectly. In New York City, Emma was on her way home. She was thinking about the beautiful engagement ring she had just chosen in the jewellery store. The stones reminded her of the intense colours of autumn leaves. At the centre of the ring was a large ruby, always a favourite stone of Emma's, encircled by diamonds and set in a gold band. Emma could not stop staring at her finger, much to the amusement of Robert, her fiancé.

The following week was cold and sunny, and the leaves were crisp underfoot. Emma loved to walk in Central Park during her lunch break. She enjoyed wrapping up warm and feeling the late autumn sun on her face. Every so often she would stop walking and take off her glove, just to peep at her ring. This had always been Emma's favourite time of year. She worked as an interior designer for a large store and was never happier than when helping customers to choose interior furnishings and inspiring them with her design ideas. The company she worked for appreciated her, and at the early age of 22 she had just been given a substantial promotion. Life was indeed very good for Emma that fall.

Autumn turned to winter and the leaves had almost gone. A sharp frost covered the ground, and the park looked like Wonderland. As she strolled through it one lunch time, Emma bought a hotdog to warm her as she made her way back to the office. She arrived back and took off her coat and gloves – and was suddenly sick with horror to discover her ruby was missing. In tears, she asked her boss if she could go back to the park to look for the stone, convinced that she must have lost it as she pulled off her gloves to buy the hotdog. Her boss suggested that first of all they should turn the glove inside out in case the ruby was caught inside. No ruby was to be found, however, and a very distraught Emma hurried back to the park.

It was like looking for the proverbial needle in a haystack. No trace of the ruby could be found. Deeply distressed, Emma rang Robert, who tried to make her feel better by telling her that they could have another ruby set into the ring. But Emma would not be consoled; she wanted her ruby back and was determined to keep searching. Fruitlessly she searched in the park each day, turning over twigs and stones and hoping the ruby would twinkle up at her at any moment.

Meanwhile, at work things were extremely busy. Christmas was fast approaching and many people were redecorating for the holiday season. Emma found herself very much in demand – which at least helped to keep her mind off the lost stone.

Christmas was only days away when Emma's mother brought down the decorations from the loft, asking Emma to help her put them up. Usually this was a job Emma loved, but this year she had no heart for anything festive. Lifting a little Christmas carrousel out of the box, Emma recalled how she had loved it as a child. She wound it up and listened in tears as it played 'Hark the Herald Angels Sing'. This was her favourite carol, and she found herself saying aloud, 'Please, angels, help me find my ruby.' This was to have been a wonderfully happy Christmas, the first of her engagement, and she had been looking forward to showing her ring to visiting relatives.

Christmas Eve dawned bright and sunny, frost twinkled along with the Christmas lights, and carols floated up from the street as Emma busied herself in the office. Looking up, she saw her boss talking to woman she recognised. Several weeks ago Emma had helped her choose furnishings for her apartment. As she beckoned Emma to join them, her boss smiled broadly. The customer greeted Emma and handed her a small plastic envelope. Twinkling inside it was the ruby. She told Emma that she had found the stone in some cream throws she had bought for the chairs. All of a sudden, Emma remembered clearly helping the customer to fold the throws and place them in bags for storage so that they would stay pristine for Christmas. The loose stone must have caught in the open-weave fabric.

At that very moment from the street below, came the strains of 'Hark the Herald Angels Sing'. Tears streamed down Emma's face. The angels heard me, she thought. A little while later she went out to find the carol singers on the street. Dropping a large donation into their collecting box, she remarked, 'That's for the angels.'

★ ★ ★

The same week that I received Emma's story, I met Carol, whose angelic encounter also involves jewellery. Carol, like many others, firmly believes that her guardian angel is a close relative who has passed on. This story revolves around Carol's daughter, who lives in Hong Kong, and some beautiful opals.

It was Carol's parents' wedding anniversary. Carol's father had given her mother, Kathleen, a set of beautiful opal jewellery. Opening the box, she was speechless at such a gift. The set comprised of necklace, earrings and bracelet, all exquisite. This did, however, present a problem for Kathleen, who was extremely superstitious. Wearing opals is considered to bring misfortune if they are not your birthstone. Beautiful as they were, she knew that she could never bring herself to wear the gems. Desperate not to offend her husband, she thanked him profusely, put the box away safely and tried to think of a solution.

Shortly after the wedding anniversary, sadly, Kathleen's husband died. Opals were the birthstone of one of Kathleen's granddaughters, so she could wear them without fear of ill luck. Carol, however, had a nagging doubt about this expensive and beautiful gift. She felt uncomfortable that Kathleen's other granddaughter, in Hong Kong, did not have a similar present.

Time passed and one day Carol's mother also died, and it fell to Carol to undertake the sad task of distributing her belongings. As she was sorting through them, Carol came across a very lovely sapphire ring and brooch. This was the answer to her problem; she could give this set of gems to her daughter in Hong Kong, redressing the balance. Over the phone she told her daughter that she had the beautiful sapphires as momentoes for her. Her daughter was thrilled.

Carol's daughter arranged to attend her grandmother's funeral. Just before she was due to arrive at the airport, Carol went to her mother's case for the jewellery – and discovered to her distress that the sapphires were missing! What could possibly have happened? Had she put them somewhere else? Knowing in her heart that this was impossible, she nevertheless frantically searched the house from top to bottom. All to no avail, there was simply no trace of the sapphires. After the funeral, Carol had to tell her daughter that the promised jewellery could not be found. Her daughter was terribly distressed and wanted no other keepsake. In her sadness, Carol even started to believe that perhaps her daughter thought she was lying. It was a very dispirited Carol that took her daughter back to the airport.

Time went on, but every time Carol spoke to her daughter on the phone she felt that the problem hung unspoken in the air. This was a source of worry and unhappiness for Carol. Since the funeral she had many times searched the little jewel case, tipping the contents out each time, half hoping to find the missing sapphires. She also searched drawers, cupboards and handbags that had belonged to Kathleen. Sadness welled up inside Carol, reaching a peak when she learnt that her daughter was coming to England once more for a visit.

The day before her daughter's arrival, Carol sat on her bed, in despair. She found herself saying out loud, 'Mother, if you are my guardian angel, will you please help me find those sapphires?' All of a sudden she was drawn back to the small case she had searched a dozen times before. But this time on lifting the lid she saw shining up at her the sapphire brooch and ring! Truly, a gift from an angel.

Incidentally, the blue of the sapphire represents the blue of heaven and symbolises truth.

Sailing off into the sunset is a dream that many of us share. For some people, however, the dream actually comes true. In the autumn of 2002, I received a letter from Katherine. Intriguingly, the address on the top was 'Yacht in transit, Zululand, Yacht Club'. Accompanying the letter was a wonderful photograph, which proved to be central to Katherine's story.

The story begins in California, where Katherine lived. She was engaged to be married and sailing around the world was a dream long shared by her and her fiancé. Determined to make it a reality, the couple started to look for a yacht to buy. California is the perfect place to look for a yacht. Sailing is a very popular pastime and many people own boats of one sort or another. There were lots of boats for sale, and as they searched, Katherine took photographs of the ones they liked, to study at home. One day a very beautiful yacht caught their eye, and Katherine took a photograph as usual. Her name was Ethereal, suggesting a celestial being or heavenly body, and Katherine thought it perfect. It appealed to her spiritual nature and she felt a deep connection with the vessel.

A meeting was arranged with the yacht's owners, and Katherine and her fiancé put in an offer. Days passed and no word came in response. Telephone messages were ignored, and they came to the conclusion that they had probably lost the yacht to another bidder, but Katherine could not shake off the feeling that somehow the yacht 'belonged' to them. At this point, Katherine' s photographs were ready for collection and she was eager to see them. Looking through the packet she came across the picture of Ethereal and, in her own words, 'came out in goosebumps'. Looking at the copy Katherine sent to me, I have to say that I too was decidedly 'goosebumped'! Above the mast, etched in bright light in a clear, azure sky was the figure of an angel incorporating a cross. To Katherine this was a sign that the boat was to be not only theirs but theirs with God's blessing.

To everyone's surprise except Katherine's, a call finally came saying that the offer had been accepted and the boat now belonged to them. For Katherine, there seemed no better place than a yacht with a celestial name and a celestial blessing to get married. Arrangements were made and Katherine and her fiancé were married on the bow of Ethereal. Following the wedding they set sail and have been sailing the world ever since.

★ ★ ★

The trees reflected in the river, they are unconscious of a spiritual world so near them. So are we.

Nathaniel Hawthorn

Four happy, healthy faces beamed out of the cover of an American magazine. Inside the magazine they explained to a reporter that they were indeed very fortunate to be so happy and healthy, for events some years previously, when they were teenagers, could have claimed the lives of all four.

It all started one very hot summer's day in Ohio, USA .The girls were trying to think of something to do that would keep them cool. As they lived close to a large lake they decided to go canoeing. They borrowed a canoe and climbed aboard feeling very excited. In retrospect they are horrified at their recklessness Not one of them could handle a canoe and none of them could swim.

The girls pushed away from the bank and paddled with difficulty, finding the craft hard to manoeuvre. They realised that even though they were not too far from the bank, the water was in fact very deep. A massive oak tree grew on the lake's edge, its branches stretching out over the water. Suddenly, as if from nowhere, a small boy appeared at the base of the tree. He called out to them loudly that the tree was about to fall and then disappeared. In disbelief they saw the giant tree start to move. It was obviously going to topple over directly onto the canoe. If it fell directly on top of them or if they were caught in the huge branches they would certainly all drown.

It was just at this point, when the tree was actually in the process of toppling over, that it appeared to halt in mid-air. Looking up in amazement, they saw the little boy re-appear. Incredibly, he was holding the whole weight of this enormous tree. He succeeded in pushing it sideways, and as it crashed into the lake, only the very tips of the branches brushed against the canoe.

It took all the girls' strength to paddle away from the sinking tree and the danger of being pulled under the water, but eventually they reached the lakeside and safety. Scrambling onto dry ground with relief, they could see no sign of the little boy who had saved them. Onlookers, and there were many, said they had not seen a boy at all during any stage of the drama, and all enquiries, with a view to offering their thanks, proved fruitless.

All four teenagers then agreed that there was no doubt: the boy could only have been an angel.

Our next story takes us to Australia, where Jenny and her family were about to enjoy the trip of a lifetime. They took off in the cold of an English winter. It was a very long flight and by the time they arrived Jenny and her brother were extremely tired. But their fatigue turned to excitement when they saw the happy crowd of aunts, uncles and cousins that had gathered to welcome them – many of whom Jenny had never met before. Among them were two fifteen-year-old – the same age as Jenny. It was clear that the holiday was going to be a lot of fun.

One of the highlights was to be a camping trip to Ayer's rock. The desert scenery was amazing – like nothing Jenny had ever seen before. The colours of the sunset and the rocks defied description. Halting at one point the caravan of family cars decanted their occupants to stretch their legs and have a cooling drink. Exploring a little distance from the road, the teenagers whooped with joy as they scrambled over rocks and scrub. For Jenny it was like being an extra in a cowboy film. Then suddenly she screamed and froze. Directly in front of her, head raised ready to pounce, was a snake. The thought flashed through her head that she was about to die, for she knew that Australia had many poisonous snakes. Her body shook with fright and she was rooted to the spot.

Then, all at once, a huge, booted foot stamped down on the snake. A large, brown hand seized it behind the head and threw it far away into the scrub. The foot belonged to a man dressed in dark green and brown walking clothes. Jenny calculated that he must have been almost seven feet tall. She sank to her knees, crying with sheer relief.

Jenny's entire family came running at this point, having heard the screams. They listened open-mouthed as Jenny told them of the snake and her rescuer. Her mother hugged her tight, but the expression on the face of her Australian uncles was one of disbelief. Where, they asked, was this huge man? If he was so tall surely they would be able to see him. There were no huge footprints on the ground and the only vehicles around belonged to them. They did, however, confirm that the snake Jenny described was poisonous and that she had indeed had a lucky escape.

Talking to her mother later, Jenny whispered, 'I know they don't believe me Mum, but truly that is exactly what happened.'

'I believe you, darling,' she said. 'I think you just met your guardian angel.'

★ ★ ★

We go to western Australia for our next story, which features a young mother called Vanessa.

Vanessa and the children (a girl of two-and-a-half and a baby) had spent a lovely weekend at Perth visiting Vanessa's mother. On Sunday Vanessa packed their things into the car and strapped the children into the back seat for the 400-km drive home. After a while they all realised they were hungry, and Vanessa stopped at a road house to buy something to eat and let her daughter run around for a while. An hour passed and Vanessa was keen to start again, anxious now to be home. Again the baby was strapped into her travel seat and the little girl safely belted in. The highway was extremely busy, full of large trucks and fast-moving traffic. Vanessa was relieved when she could turn off the very busy road and take a little used short-cut. Feeling safer, Vanessa told her small daughter it would now be all right for her to sit in the front seat. The little girl scrambled over the seat, was strapped in and off they went. At this point the baby started to cry loudly and, glancing over her shoulder, Vanessa saw that she had dropped her bottle.

Since the road was deserted, Vanessa was driving faster than usual, wanting to get home quickly. Without slowing down, she turned to retrieve the bottle for her baby daughter. This took no more than a couple of seconds but, to Vanessa's horror, when she turned round, she found herself on the opposite side of the road. In her panic she over-corrected, with the result that they catapulted back across the road, heading for the steep ditch on the other side. They were travelling too fast to stop in time to avoid the ditch. The car suddenly became air-borne, and as they left the road Vanessa found herself saying, 'Help me, Nan.' This was the name she used for her grandmother who had died three years previously and to whom she had felt very close.

Vanessa tried to focus on where the car was heading while she held on to her daughter in the front seat with her arm protectively across her chest. Just then, directly in her line of vision, she saw the face of her nan. The face was incredibly clear and could not have been mistaken for anyone or anything else. Her nan was smiling and radiating comfort.

The car landed upright, hitting a large tree as it did so. The force of the impact and the angle of the vehicle resulted in the complete collapse of the side of car where the little girl had been sitting. Had she not climbed into the front passenger seat she would certainly have been killed. As Vanessa quickly pulled the girls from the car, she was joined by a passer-by – a rare event in itself on that road – who rushed to see if help was needed. He had already called the police and ambulance on seeing what looked like a very serious accident. However, none of the family had as much as a scratch, a fact the police and ambulance crew found hard to believe. Vanessa has no doubt at all, that her nan was her guardian angel that day.

Miriam had lived in Cape Town all her life. She belonged to a large, close-knit family, and had a great circle of friends and a job she enjoyed immensely. Life was sunny for her in every sense of the word. Liz was Miriam's much loved sister, only twelve months her senior at nineteen, and the girls had been best friends as well as sisters from childhood. Their interest were very different, however. Liz was very keen on sport and hoped to work in the sports industry after leaving university. Miriam had always been keen on computer technology and enjoyed her job with a large IT company.

Arriving at the office early one morning to avoid the traffic, Miriam poured herself a cup of coffee. As she sipped it, she gazed out of the window. The traffic did seem to be very heavy that morning, and the car park was quickly filling as other workers arriving for the day. Miles away, she jumped when the phone rang on her desk. Later she would be grateful that she had sat down to take the call, because her world was suddenly to come crashing down around her. It was her mother calling from the hospital. Liz had been struck by a fast-moving car. She was seriously injured and had been rushed to surgery, but there was little hope that she would pull through. Her mother urged Miriam to make her way to the hospital as quickly as possible. Knowing that there was a taxi rank nearby and in no fit state of mind to drive, Miriam ran as fast as she could to get a taxi.

Leaping into the cab, she asked breathlessly to be taken to the hospital as quickly as possible. Suddenly she was aware that there was in fact already a young woman inside. She touched Miriam's arm comfortingly. 'Not to worry,' she said, 'I'm going to the hospital too, so we can share the cab.' Gratefully, Miriam sank into the seat and smiled at the woman. She can't be much older than me, she thought, but she has such an air of maturity about her. Miriam found herself telling the woman about the events of the morning. Listening intently, she nodded her head and held Miriam's hand. Her touch was cool and confident, and Miriam found herself thinking how very beautiful she was.

At last they arrived at the hospital and together they walked down the drive, the young woman still holding Miriam's hand. As they reached the large front door, the woman said in a very determined voice, 'You must not worry. I know your sister will not die and all will be well.' She then gave Miriam a gentle push towards the door. Walking through the door first, Miriam held it open for her new friend. But as she turned towards her, she caught her breath with shock, there was no one behind her! The long driveway was completely empty. How could this possibly be? There was no time to ponder this event though. Miriam rushed to the area where her mother sat silently crying, waiting for her. The feeling of calm and confidence still filled Miriam, and she put her arms around her mother, telling her with conviction that Liz would be fine.

Liz is now home and well, having survived the surgery and made a faster recovery than anyone could have thought possible. The young woman in the taxi with her warm words and smile are still etched on Miriam's memory. When she eventually had time to sit down and think about the events of that morning, she came to the only possible conclusion: she had been comforted by an angel.

The following stories reached me from Philadelphia, a part of the USA that experiences blizzards in abundance each winter. It appears that many people have their guardian angel present in such conditions.

Melissa loves American football and is a keen fan of the Philadelphia Eagles. Her dearest wish was to own an Eagles jacket with their emblem emblazoned on the back. These jackets, however, are very expensive. Her parents, worried about the cost, resisted the idea of buying one for quite some time. Eventually, however, they capitulated and bought Melissa the longed-for jacket as an early Christmas gift. They had to admit that it was both warm and practical. Thickly padded against the cold, it made Melissa feel very snug. The weather was turning cold and, with just a few weeks to go to Christmas, the snow fell thickly. Shouts of excitement could be heard as children ran outside to play in the fresh, deep snow.

Melissa's mother, Joyce, smiled as her daughter eagerly pulled on her beloved jacket and, with eyes shining, dragged her sled outside. The house was on top of a hill, and Joyce called to Melissa that she would pop into a neighbour's house for a moment before coming outside to watch her sledge down. But, when Joyce came out of the house, Melissa was nowhere to be seen. She had simply vanished. Concern mounting, Joyce started off down the hill, only too aware that a busy main road joined their street at the bottom. Calling Melissa's name, she started to run, fear gripping her throat.

Her worst fears were realised when she reached the bottom of the hill, where panicked onlookers told her that Melissa had fallen under a car and was being dragged at speed along the main road. It appeared that a neighbour had driven down the hill, unaware that Melissa had slid underneath the vehicle and that her jacket had caught on the car's frame. The road was very busy and the traffic was moving very quickly. The ice was thick and Melissa was sliding along at tremendous speed.

Pedestrians and motorists, who could see Melissa's head and shoulders sticking out under the car, shouted at the driver to stop, but they went unheard in the traffic's roar. Joyce was running as fast as she could and yelling at the top of her voice for someone to halt the car. Many people joined her and there was soon a crowd of people running after the car, completely helpless to prevent the horror unfolding before their eyes. At last, mercifully, a driver travelling in the opposite direction grasped the situation and moved with lightning speed. He swerved his car into the path of the oncoming car in an effort to stop it, in the process turning his own car over. Thankfully he was unhurt and at last the speeding car screeched to a halt. The man emerged from his upturned car and yelled at the other driver that a child was caught underneath her car. Ashen-faced, she jumped from her car in disbelief.

At this point Melissa's distraught mother finally caught up with the car, at the same time that the police arrived at the scene, having been alerted by passing drivers. Swiftly they extricated Melissa from the car frame and took her to the police station, where medical help was available. Incredible as it may seem, however, although her beloved jacket was torn to shreds, the clothes beneath the jacket were also torn to shreds, and even her underwear was in shreds, Melissa did not have one scratch on her body! There was only one small bruise to show for her terrifying ordeal.

When she had recovered a little, Melissa told her mother and the police that she remembered absolutely nothing after the initial fall that had catapulted her underneath the car. She was aware of the thick ice underneath her and a heavy weight on her chest and then she blacked out. The police, however, were totally baffled; they simply could not understand how Melissa had undergone such an ordeal and emerged unscathed. They would normally expect serious, if not fatal, injuries to have been sustained in such an accident.

The incident became the talking point of Philadelphia. Television and radio stations and all the newspapers were captivated by the story, which became known as 'the Christmas miracle'. The Eagles, on hearing the story, presented Melissa with a brand-new jacket, with their love. But still no one had any explanation for the miracle.

No one, that is, except Melissa's parents. They firmly believe that Melissa had two very special angels looking after her. Both of Melissa's grandmothers had died some time before. They had adored Melissa, and she had been very close to them both. Melissa's parents have no doubt that the two women were guarding her in an angelic capacity. They are sure she is being watched over still.

★ ★ ★

Melissa has an Aunt Connie, who happens to be a friend of mine and was keen for me to hear the story of her niece. Anyone who has read my book *Angels and Miracles* will be aware of how important angels have been in Connie's life and in the lives of her family. She recalls another amazing story from her school days.

Like Melissa, Connie lives in Philadelphia. When she was young, she had two classmates who were identical twin girls, with long blonde hair and strikingly pretty. One day one of the twin sisters was very tearful in class. The teacher asked her what was wrong. The little girl replied that she had been upset by a very vivid dream the night before. In it an angel appeared and told her, 'Fear not, for I shall be with you.' It did seem like an odd thing to say to a little girl, and so the teacher assured her it was simply a strange dream. Still confused about why she should have had such a strange and vivid dream, nevertheless the girl took the teacher's advice and decided to try to put it out of her mind.

Walking home from school that day, the little girl was hit by a car and killed instantly. Connie could only conclude that the angel had warned her, telling her not to be frightened because she would be there waiting for her.

★ ★ ★

Our next story is also set in the USA and concerns a boy called Buddy. Buddy was thrilled to be appointed an altar boy at the age of nine years. The following Sunday would be his first service in his new capacity and he took this duty very seriously.

The large church was only a short walk away, but on Saturday night it started snowing and on Sunday morning the snow was still falling fast. Despite this, Buddy set out for the church, reasoning that it was not very far and he would be perfectly safe. However, the journey was far from easy and by the time he reached the church the snow was almost two feet deep. To his disappointment, he found a notice on the church door saying that the service had been cancelled. Wearily he turned and tried to retrace his steps homewards. The normally, short, pleasant walk now became an ordeal. Buddy ploughed through the deepening snow, feeling swamped by the size of the snow drifts.

Suddenly an extremely large man, his face almost covered by a scarf, loomed in front of Buddy. In one easy movement, he picked up the boy and placed him onto his shoulders. Buddy felt no fear, only relief and a sense of safety. No words were spoken and, without being told where Buddy lived, the man walked straight to his home, placing him gently down by his front door. At this point the young boy was relieved and bemused in equal measures. He turned to say 'thank you' to his rescuer but, to his astonishment, there was no one in sight. Even stranger, there wasn't a footprint to be seen in the snow. The long path leading to Buddy's front door and the entire pavement beyond were as soft and even as when the snow first fell.

★ ★ ★

Our next amazing encounter took place in the American city of Detroit. This city also endures severe winter weather and driving is often extremely dangerous. The highways were covered with snow as Linda cautiously drove home. It was just before Christmas 2001 and the snowstorm was quickly building into one of dangerous proportions. The road was one huge sheet of ice and Linda could feel her car slipping on this treacherous surface. Visibility was almost zero and Linda was feeling very afraid.

Without warning, a huge tractor and trailer began to overtake her car. There was obviously insufficient room. On either side of the highway loomed high concrete walls, and as Linda tried to move away from the truck she found herself right up against one of them, but there was simply nothing she could do about it. With horror, she saw the tractor, obviously out of control, begin to slide on the ice, heading straight towards her. She did the only thing she could in the circumstances – pray hard!

Suddenly, before her astonished gaze, a huge angel appeared directly in front of her car. Seemingly made of snow and ice crystals, it was at least 10 feet tall, its glistening wings spread majestically to a huge span. Watching mesmerised, Linda saw the angel float swiftly down between her car and the tractor. It placed one massive hand on each vehicle and completely covered Linda's car with one massive wing, cloaking it protectively. The vehicles were gently prised away from each other and the tractor guided safely back into its own lane. As quickly as it had taken shape, the angel dissolved once more into the swirling snow flakes. A modern-day miracle if ever there was one, Linda says. She thanks God for saving her life by sending his angel in answer to her prayer on that desperately dangerous night.

Cyprus is not known for snow and ice, in fact generally just the opposite: blue skies and sunshine. Michelle went to live in Cyprus because her fiancé was stationed there with the British army. It was a big move and she wondered if she had really done the right thing. One day, when she was alone at home, she noticed the most wonderful fragrance, although there was no apparent source for it. Eventually she decided that this was a sign that she had been right to join her fiancé.

Michelle's job involved a 60-mile drive each day, so she depended on her car a great deal. One day, just as she was about to drive home, she realised it was leaking huge amounts of oil. To her horror she saw that the thick oil had spilled all over the engine. She cleaned it off with difficulty, and a friend drove her to the nearest garage to buy more, then with some trepidation she set off for home. The journey was uneventful but on arrival she discovered that she had lost a treasured gold ring, a gift from her brother. It must have slipped off my finger when I was cleaning up the oil, she thought sadly. The next problem was the discovery that she had lost her door key. 'It really has been one of those days,' she said aloud.

When she arrived at work the following morning, she asked, with very little hope, whether anyone had seen the ring or the key. To her delight, a colleague had found the ring on the floor of a very busy reception area. At the end of the day, before setting out for home, she once more checked the oil. Lifting the bonnet of her car, she saw, to her amazement, the keys sitting on top of the engine. That small bunch keys had sat on the car engine for over sixty miles and not fallen off. At this point Michelle was convinced that she was being watched over.

On returning home to England when the posting ended, Michelle married her fiancé and happily resumed her life close to friends and family. All was well until one day she had to attend hospital for some tests. Feeling anxious, Michelle asked her mother if she could accompany her. She agreed, but then, just before the appointment, rang to say that unfortunately could not be with her. Michelle put down the telephone and began to sob. Suddenly she looked up to see a beautiful, soft white feather float down to land on the desk directly in front of her. In no doubt this time, Michelle dried her eyes and thanked her angel.

'I'm definitely going to India!' The dinner conversation ceased abruptly and all eyes turned towards Ellie.

'So you won't be going to school tomorrow, then?' her mother asked with a twinkle in her eye. The family burst into laughter, but Ellie was undaunted.

'I didn't mean I would be going tomorrow,' she said in a firm voice, 'but I am going to save and one day I shall go!'

Ellie was only fourteen, and there was to be a lot of saving and a long wait ahead before she would achieve her ambition. She was not quite sure herself why she was so keen to see India. True, she had a close friend at school who was Indian, and her stories of the country fascinated Ellie. But the urge to go, she believed, went deeper. She was determined to see India one day.

At the age of twenty, Ellie decided that she was at last in a position to travel to India. Seeing a good deal on a package tour in her local travel agents, she booked the trip of a lifetime. This would be Ellie's first major holiday and her first trip abroad.

When she arrived, the sights, sounds and taste of India were a feast for her senses, and she loved every aspect of this amazing country. It was everything she had hoped for. While staying in one very beautiful hotel, Ellie met a fascinating couple from America. Michael was half Indian and half American. He had been born in India but had lived in the United States for many years, where he had clearly prospered. His wife was American – a lovely warm character called Rita. Visually they made an odd pair and were often teased, for Michael was six foot eight inches tall and Rita only five foot! But there was something about this couple that drew Ellie to them, and all three became instant friends. When it became time for them to go their separate ways, they had exchanged addresses and telephone numbers with Ellie, assuring her that should she visit the United States, she would be a very welcome at their home. Michael said that she had now become part of their karma. Ellie knew deep down that there was a very special bond between them and felt certain that she would visit them one day.

Sad to say goodbye to her new friends, Ellie moved on, three days later finding herself in the large city of Bombay with all its hustle and bustle. She had made friends with two other young women in her tour party, and they stayed closely together in the busy streets. One day they were shopping for fabric. Material of all kinds spilled out in front of them, and they were amazed and fascinated by the wonderful colours. Examining a sari length of fabulous cloth, Ellie asked the shopkeeper about the price. Eventually agreeing on a sum, she bought the cloth and said her goodbyes. Turning around she was horrified to find that her friends were nowhere in sight. The streets were so crowded that Ellie could not see beyond a few feet in front of her. Panic rose in her throat and she tried not to cry.

Darting about in several directions, hoping to catch up with the other two, she soon realised that it was a hopeless task. To make the matter worse, in her panic she could not remember where their hotel was or the name of it. At the point of despair and with tears rolling down her face, she suddenly saw a wonderful sight. There, only a short distance ahead was Michael, her American friend. It was not difficult to spot him, at his height he was head and shoulders above the crowd. There was no mistaking him and Ellie, sighing with relief, hurried after him. Try as she might, she simply could not catch up, the crowds were so tightly packed. Michael, however, stood out like a moving flag pole and she followed as best she could. Eventually they came to an open square and the crowds thinned out. With a cry of joy, Ellie saw her two friends and rushed to join them. They had been very worried and had searched for her as best they could when they realised she was no longer following them. Happily they made their way back to the hotel together.

Ellie told her two friends how lucky she had been to spot Michael in the crowd, adding that if it had not been seen him she had no idea what she would have done. Her friends agreed that she had been lucky but added that they had had no idea Michael and Rita (whom they had also met) were travelling to Bombay; they had not mentioned the fact. 'Maybe they changed their schedule,' Ellie replied – because there was no doubt about it, she had seen Michael in that crowd; it was impossible to confuse him with anyone else!

Finally, after a wonderful holiday, Ellie arrived home, laden with gifts. She told her mother the story of how she had got lost and been rescued by Michael and asked her whether she could ring the couple at their home in Miami. Michael and Rita were thrilled to hear from Ellie. Mentioning the incident in Bombay, Ellie asked Michael, 'Don't you think that amazing?'

'I find it miraculous,' Michael replied, 'because we flew home the morning after you left for Bombay and were back home in Miami when you say you saw me.'

Ellie was speechless, quite at a loss for an explanation. Michael, however, continued, 'There are more things on heaven and earth than we recognise, and, after, all didn't I tell you that you are now part of our karma?'

Ellie's mother had a different explanation: 'I may not know much about karma, but I do think you encountered your guardian angel, in the guise of Michael to make sure that you would see and follow him.'

Chapter 5

I Know My Angel

'Tis only when they spring to heaven
That angels reveal themselves to you.

Robert Browning

Many people tell me, especially when they have been dramatically rescued, that they know for certain who their angel was. A dearly loved grandmother, or grandfather, is often seen in the guise of an angel, the bond of protective love unbroken even by death. Close relatives and close friends also often appear as angels. Even if we don't actually see our rescuing angel, the feeling of knowing can be very strong. The theologian and philosopher Emanuel Swedenborg stated that the reason we are here in the first place is to train to become angels. Love is the very essence of our being and transcends death. The experiences in this chapter tell how lives are saved and people are comforted by angels they already know.

'I'm going to the party with Steve,' announced Jane, with a huge smile.

Her friend punched the air and yelled, 'Yes, result!'

They both laughed. Jane had been very keen on Steve for quite a while; now at last he had picked up this fact and asked her out. The occasion was a birthday party for a mutual friend. Jane would know lots of people there, but, most importantly, she would be with Steve.

Steve had passed his driving test at the age of seventeen, but it was only now, two years later, that he could afford to buy a car. 'Freedom at last!' he said as he took delivery of it. Although in the meantime his mother had let him borrow her car occasionally, nevertheless his experience behind the wheel was limited

The party – a barbecue – took place on a lovely warm summer night in late June. Jane was wearing a new outfit and was feeling very excited. Steve picked her up in his lovely new car. The party venue was a friend's large back garden. It was lit by torches and fairly lights, and music filled the air. Wonderful food and plenty to drink completed the atmosphere, and everyone had a wonderful time. In the early hours of the morning, the guests began to leave, and Steve, who said he was feeling a little unwell, suggested that they should also go home. Saying goodbye and thank you, they walked to the front of the house and down the street to the parking spot where the car had been left for the evening.

Jane began to worry, it was obvious that Steve had drunk far too much. As they walked to the car he swerved from side to side. Jane knew he should certainly not drive. At the suggestion that they return to the house and call a taxi, Steve became angry, declaring himself perfectly capable of driving. Purposefully he opened the car door and indicated that Jane should get in. Much against her better judgement and at a loss what to do, she climbed in the passenger seat, but she was trembling with fear. Silently she muttered, 'If I have a guardian angel, please help!'

Steve turned the key in the ignition, but the car did not start. Grumbling, he turned the key again, but there was no response, not even a noise to indicate something amiss. 'This is just does not make sense,' he said. 'It was perfectly all right when we drove here earlier.' The car was suddenly surrounded by a white mist, and Steve said, 'Fog, that's all we need.'

A warm tingling sensation spread over Jane's back as she peered into the white mist. Slowly a face emerged. It was her grandmother's, smiling at her and looking exactly has she had done when alive. Mesmerised, Jane said to Steve, 'Can you see anybody out there?'

'No,' he answered aggressively. 'What are you talking about?' Realising that only she could see her grandmother, Jane decided to keep silent.

With great irritation, Steve announced that they would have to go back to the house after all and get a taxi. Breathing a sigh of relief Jane quickly left the car, noticing the face and the mist had rapidly vanished.

After the taxi had dropped her safely home, Jane sat in bed pondering the events of the night. My grandmother must be my guardian angel, she thought. Only she could have prevented the car from starting. She literally saved my life, of that I'm sure. Saying 'thank you' to her grandmother angel, she snuggled down in bed, feeling once more the warm, tingling sensation.

What about Steve? you might ask. Well, the next day, he returned to pick up the car. It started first time of course. He rang Jane to tell her this and also to apologise for being drunk. 'I will never drink and drive again,' he promised her, adding, 'How lucky we were that the car wouldn't start.' Luck, thought Jane, had absolutely nothing to do with it!

Granddad Durose must have been great fun. His granddaughter Stephanie recalls talking to truckers on his CB radio and listening to country and western music with him. They enjoyed each other's company and were very close. As a child Stephanie knew how loved she was, and she was terribly upset when, after falling in the shower, her grandfather died of a blood clot. It was a great shock. No one in the family could have predicted losing such an active and lively grandfather in this way.

Feeling low after the funeral, Stephanie's family decided a treat might cheer them up, so the following weekend they decided to go to Blackpool. Anyone who has ever visited this lively seaside town will tell you it's impossible to stay miserable there for very long. For children it's a magical place – there's so much for them to see and do – and adults enjoy it for its gaudy fun. Stephanie and her brother had spent a glorious day on the pleasure beach, with its rollercoaster rides and funfair attractions. Then, in high spirits, the family strolled along the sea front, oblivious to the danger that lay ahead. A little distance ahead, a group of boys looking for trouble had broken into a car with the intention of spending the afternoon joyriding.

Crossing the road, the family found themselves directly in the path of this speeding car, as it hurtled around a corner. Instinctively they ran to safety – all, that is, except for Stephanie. She says that to this day she has no idea why she let go of her mother's hand and stood still in the middle of the road. It's not uncommon, however, to find yourself rooted to the spot with fear, and perhaps this was what happened to Stephanie. Whatever the reason, there she was in the path of a speeding car, driven by under-age joy riders with no idea how to control it. Bombarded by shouts of fear and instructions to run, Stephanie remained immobile. She felt as if she was in her own little world and can recall no sound at all. Indeed, she felt oddly calm.

Then, at the last moment, the car screeched to a halt, miraculously stopping with its front tires against her knees! A firm hand was placed into Stephanie's and she was gently led to the side of the road and out of danger. The police were quickly on the scene and expressed astonishment that the boys had managed to stop the car so quickly. Firstly, it had been travelling at tremendous speed; secondly, the boys were under-age and had no idea how to stop it; and, thirdly, an under-age driver would normally panic and lose whatever control he had.

But the biggest mystery was who had held Stephanie's hand. No one witnessing the event saw anyone approach her, but Stephanie insisted to her mother that she had been led to safety. Eventually, Stephanie connected the almost fatal accident with the death of her grandfather only days before. She is convinced that her grandfather took her hand and led her to safety.

Many incidents have occurred since in Stephanie's life that confirm for her that her guardian grandfather is still close by. She feels blessed and is grateful for this wonderful angel.

Angels communicate with us in myriad ways. Sometimes a very gentle contact is all we need to comfort us, but at other times a more intense or dramatic contact is necessary. The latter was the case for Ann-Marie and her family. Her story is tragic and moving but also very beautiful. Here is how it all happened.

One weekend, Ann-Marie's fourteen-year-old daughter Lianne asked if she could sleep at her friend's house. Ann-Marie gave her permission, but with a little reluctance and an unease she could not fully explain. The friends enjoyed a great Saturday evening together, but on Sunday morning they found themselves at a bit of a loose end. It was a sunny, fresh, spring day in March, so they went out for a walk. Eventually they met up with some friends and they all sat on a wall, chatting – two boys and three girls, full of beans and rather bored.

One boy noticed that the wall they were sitting on surrounded a derelict, industrial building. He decided it would be fun to explore, and so, glad to have found something to do, the rest followed. One thing led to another, and before long they were climbing on the roof. Lianne was usually a very sensible and mature teenager, but the sense of adventure was infectious and so she joined in the fun. The two boys were ahead of Lianne when suddenly the fun faded as they realised the roof was unsafe. They called out to Lianne go back. They are unsure if she heard them, as, within seconds, a skylight collapsed, hurling Lianne to the floor. An ambulance was called and Lianne was put on a life support system, but despite every effort to save her, Lianne died.

We can only imagine the distress and pain her family endured. Ann-Marie was expecting another baby at the time and must have felt she was in an emotional spin-dryer. Somehow, though, she, Lianne's father, Jose, and Lianne's older brother, Christian, struggled on from hour to hour. They decided to donate Lianne's organs, in the hope that others would live on through their daughter.

The day after Lianne's death, Ann-Marie felt her presence all day. Desperately wishing to be alone at one point, Ann-Marie went into her daughter's bedroom and lay on the bed. She found herself praying that this was not in fact the end, that there was another life awaiting her daughter. Then she heard a voice. It spoke to her confirming that this was true and that Lianne was not alone but embarking on a journey of discovery. A wonderful, bright, glowing light surrounded Anne-Marie's body and she felt incredible peace flood through her.

The new baby was born, bringing happiness amid the grief. He was called Thomas, a name that Lianne had chosen before she died. The family decided to go on the holiday they had planned, hoping that the rest would be helpful. When they arrived home again, Christian received his examination results. They were excellent. So much was good in their lives. How they wished Lianne could have shared in all of it.

But there were signs that Lianne was not in fact all that far away. Emanating from Lianne's bedroom was a very strong fragrance that pervaded the whole upper floor of the house. It was Lianne's favourite perfume, which she wore often. Could this be a communication from Lianne? The family felt uplifted by the possibility.

Other signs revealed themselves. One day Jose was riding home on a local tram. Looking through the window, he saw a distinctly angel-shaped cloud. It felt like a message specifically for him. The cloud remained throughout his journey home, appearing to simply 'hang' motionless in the sky, not changing in shape or density.

Just before her birthday, Lianne's grandmother also felt Lianne's presence, accompanied by the wonderful fragrance. For her, this was a sign that Lianne was thinking about her at this special time. The birthday, coupled with Thomas's christening on the 8th of October, was an occasion for all the family to get together. The extended family also attended and the garden was filled with people. Once more Lianne's fragrance filled her room, and this time followed her mother out into the garden, where all present noticed the lovely smell.

It is actually very unusual for a fragrant contact to be present on several occasions, but this was the case for Lianne's family. On Ann-Marie's birthday, two days after the christening, the fragrance followed her into every room of the house, and even outdoors when she drove to the shops. So strong was her daughter's presence that Ann-Marie found herself reading her own birthday cards and Thomas's christening cards aloud, sharing them with her daughter. For the whole following week, the fragrance was present and noticed by the whole family.

There was one more sign. In Lianne's bedroom was a clock with a pendulum that usually only worked sporadically. At this point, however, the pendulum started to move spontaneously and began to swing ferociously when Jose was in the room. The family gathered in the bedroom and Jose played his guitar, joining them all together in music.

The urge to keep a loved one's bedroom exactly as it has always been can be very strong. When two and a half years had passed since the death of their daughter, Lianne's parents decided that Thomas needed a space of his own. Ann-Marie felt sure that Lianne would have loved her little brother to have her room. Feeling sure they were doing the right thing, Jose started work on redecorating the bedroom. All day long Lianne's special fragrance filled the room, telling him she was in fact delighted. How marvellous for the family to have this ongoing and close contact with their angel daughter.

It is now three years since the family lost their daughter. Christian is at university. Thomas is a bundle of fun and keeps his parents on their toes. Lianne visits less and less, knowing that the family will move on with their lives. Nevertheless, the entire family feel she is never far away and will be with them always. Nothing can take away the closeness that binds the earthly family to their angel daughter – or the belief that one day they will be reunited.

Sitting in my bedroom on the floor
I sometimes wonder
Why I was put on this earth.
Was It for a reason
Or am I just another face in the crowd?
I shout it out aloud.
Is there a reason why I am here?
I do have a family we all care,
But sometimes like others I am all alone.

Lianne Marie Gomez

I am sure you have heard about children who have imaginary friends. Perhaps you even had one yourself. Previous generations often explained the phenomenon as the result of a vivid imagination or of loneliness. Today, some people believe that small children are much closer to the angels and are in fact playing with angel children or talking to angel adults, who are simply invisible to us.

Lucy could often be heard chatting away to someone only she could see. This 'friend' appeared to her in her bedroom and, although she told her family that a man appeared in her room, she was quite unafraid.

One bonfire night, Lucy and her family were in their garden enjoying the fireworks, Lucy chatting away to her invisible friend about the bonfire and the fun they were all having. Her family were rather perplexed about this 'man' who was now at Lucy's side in the garden. Taking Lucy gently indoors, her mum asked her to describe him. A very detailed description followed. Lucy didn't know the word for a moustache, but she tried to describe one all the same. Her mother smiled. Later, she told the rest of the family what Lucy had said. Open-mouthed, they all instantly agreed that the description perfectly fitted her great-grandfather. He had, of course, died long before Lucy was born!

At the age of sixteen Linda had a near death experience. After this it would seem that she had a heightened spiritual awareness which has stayed with her throughout her life. Vivid dreams have played a big part in this, providing comfort and reassurance in times of stress. Many people experience dreams featuring people they have lost. This is a way that the dead can contact us without causing fear. These contact dreams are so vivid that they feel real and even many years later remain crystal-clear in the memory. These dreams remain ever near the surface of memory, allowing instant recall.

Linda was living in Portugal when her mother died, and she felt a huge sense of loneliness as well as grief at not having had the opportunity to say goodbye. Six months passed and Easter was approaching. Linda decided to fly home to be with her father. She rang him several times, and was puzzled that he didn't answer the phone. Eventually, she discovered that he was in fact undergoing a fairly minor operation in hospital. He had asked the family not to tell her about the operation. He knew he would soon be home and did not want to worry her.

Relieved to hear that this operation was only minor, Linda said that she would return home to look after him on his discharge from hospital, much to the delight of her family. Sadly, however, this was not to be. Before Linda could fly home, she received a telephone call to say that her father had died unexpectedly. This was a dreadful shock for her. Yet again a dearly loved parent had died without her being able to say goodbye. Linda was enveloped by a cloud of sadness. Nothing, it seemed, could penetrated the gloom. Her friends and family were worried about her, but did not know how to help.

Then one night Linda had an amazing dream which would transform her life. The dream began with Linda walking through a beautiful wood and emerging in a sunny meadow. On the edge of the meadow stood a small white fence. This seemed to have a symbolic meaning, as if she could go no further. In the distance, at the edge of the meadow, a group of people were clearly visible. All of them were dressed in white and Linda felt waves of love and joy emanating from them. Seated in the centre of this group, she was sure she recognised her mother. This person was looking directly at her and there was a feeling of familiarity. Someone emerged from the group and began to walk towards Linda. As this figure approached, she realised that it was a man and he was not in fact wearing a white gown but a grey suit. It was her father, dressed in clothes she instantly recognised.

What a delight it was for Linda to see him looking happy and well. He gave her a wonderful smile as he came to a halt by the little white fence. The message Linda received was simple and to the point: 'I'm all right, we're all right.'

After this dream, Linda says, her life turned around instantly. 'How I wish everyone could have such an experience,' she told me. For Linda the question 'Is there life after death?' has been well and truly answered.

If you have read my book *Children and Angels*, you will probably remember Thomas. When Thomas was still a baby, he lost his father. However, this experience has given him tremendous insight into death and loss – which may just be the reason why Thomas is a guardian angel. Hard to believe? You might think so, but perhaps you will change your mind when you have read his story.

Amanda, Thomas's mum, has been a diabetic since the age of twelve. As you can imagine this added to the stress Amanda faced when trying to come to terms with the death of her husband and the care of a young baby. Thomas was very ill himself as a newborn, so Amanda's life was not easy. One day she noticed a very odd coincidence. Feeling unwell with associated symptoms of her diabetes, she heard Thomas crying particularly lustily. By the time she had got to his cot, however, he was again fast asleep. This sequence of events happened again and again. Whenever Amanda felt the onset of symptoms, Thomas cried. There did not seem to be any explanations for this, since he was usually in another room, making it impossible for him to simply pick up his mother's feelings.

Today, Thomas is nine years old and life is settled and happy for him and Amanda. He has a loving stepfather and a lovely little sister. One serious problem remains, however: Amanda's diabetes has taken a sinister turn for the worst. When a serious situation is about to develop, she has no warning symptoms that she is about to become dangerously ill. It appears that she has lost the ability to recognise when an attack may occur. This is particularly dangerous because the onset is usually at night, when Amanda is asleep. She explains, 'I would simply fall into a coma from which I wouldn't awake.' What has saved Amanda is the remarkable fact is that each time this happens, Thomas shouts loudly for his mum, sometimes even going into her bedroom to ensure she wakes. Amanda is then able to take the necessary steps to avert the onset of a coma.

Incredibly, on most of the occasions when Thomas has aroused Amanda, she has gone to his bedroom to find him fast asleep! She still has no notion how he knows she is falling into a coma. Even on those occasions when he has appeared at her bedside, there was no visible sign that could indicate to him that she was becoming ill. There is no sound to warn of her condition either, and, in any case, Thomas's bedroom is the farthest away from his parents' in a large house. How does he save his mother's life time after time? His mother and stepfather are convinced that the warning comes from his daddy in heaven, prompting Thomas to act as his mother's guardian angel. Knowing only too well that angels come in all shapes and sizes, I have to agree.

Many of us respond to the always changing beauty of trees. For Bethany, however, trees have a very special significance . When she was just twelve years old her father was diagnosed with incurable cancer. The family was, of course, devastated. After twelve months of great distress, her father died, and Bethany found the pain very hard to cope with, for she had loved her father very much. She especially missed working in the garden with him. They would plant flowers and vegetables and she had her very own little patch to look after. At the very bottom of the garden was a huge oak tree, with a swing for Bethany and her brother to play on. How she loved that tree swing! She would spend many an hour idly swinging there. If she became bored with gardening she would simply sit and swing, watching her father work. Those days, she thought, are gone forever, and her tears flowed fast.

Now it was spring again, and the oak was in leaf, but this year there was no joy in that for Bethany. It was three months since her father's death and she still missed him very much. Waking one sunny morning, Bethany recalled a vivid dream she had had during the night. Her father had been with her walking in woodlands, pointing out the different types of trees and telling her all would be well. Now, lying in bed, she could still feel the warm comfortable feeling of love coming from her father. For the first time since his death she felt a real sense of calm, and the hope that eventually she could move on without pain. She decided that she would plant some flowers in her own little patch of garden.

Later that day, as the sun was setting, Bethany filled the watering can and went to give her new plants a soaking. As she walked down the garden path she suddenly stopped in her tracks. There standing under the oak tree was her father! She did not call out, did not even move, for fear that he would disappear. No words were spoken. He smiled lovingly at his daughter, and she recalls thinking that there seemed to be a light coming from his figure, almost like a torch beam. Slowly the vision faded, and Bethany walked down the path to the oak tree in a daze. There was no trace of what she had seen, although she really did not know what she might expect to be there. The oak tree, as you might imagine, is now Bethany's favourite place to sit. Not only does she have all those happy memories to share with the mighty oak but she knows her father is very close.

Most of you reading this will not remember the Falklands war. The Falkland Islands are situated off the southernmost tip of South America in the south Atlantic. Back in the 1980s, Argentina demanded they should no longer be under the rule of Great Britain and attempted an invasion. Britain reacted by declaring war. It was a tense and difficult time for everyone involved, especially those families on both sides who saw their young sons and daughters leave to fight for their country. The following is a remarkable story about a young man who lost his life in the Falklands. It was told to me by Barry, a friend of the family.

The young man concerned was a communications officer and was dispatched to repair a communications post on a steep mountain in South Georgia, one of the islands involved in the conflict. Conditions were less than favourable and a terrible accident occurred. The young soldier fell down the mountain and lost his life. It was a dreadful blow to the family, and he was badly missed, especially by his brother.

One morning, long after the war had ceased, the young man's brother was driving to work in heavy traffic. All of a sudden he lost control of his Ford Capri and ploughed into a tree with considerable force. On the opposite side of the road, an AA man witnessed this dreadful accident. He ran to a garage close by to ring for the emergency services, telling the operator and the garage staff that there were two young men in the car, one of them in army uniform. The emergency services swiftly reached the scene. They were, however, confused to find that there was only one man inside the car! The AA man could not believe this. He had, he said, distinctly seen another young man in army uniform.

Sadly, the brother lost his life in this accident. It's difficult to imagine the grief of the family at losing another son, but perhaps they were comforted by the knowledge that their sons were now together. People nearing death frequently tell of being met by loved ones. How wonderful for that young man to be met by his own brother, a guardian angel in uniform.

You may be thinking that a guardian angel in military uniform is unique. You would be wrong. No sooner had the last story reached me than I heard of another such angel.

Many people only discover their guardian angel in a time of great stress. Some people meet their angel once in a lifetime, others two or three times. Some fortunate people, however, have been accompanied by their angel since they were a very small child. One such person is Nadine, a quietly spoken, serene and self-assured girl. Many incidents occurred throughout her childhood to indicate that she was being looked after by an angel. Once, as a very small child, while she was playing in a sandpit she believed that she had seen a seahorse. An unlikely creature to find in a sandpit for sure, and Nadine says now that obviously there was no such creature there, but something had to attract her attention. The seahorse leapt from the sandpit and Nadine followed to catch it. In that second, the heavy wooden lid above the pit fell down and would without doubt have killed the little girl.

Some time later, while playing in the grounds of the farm where she lived, Nadine noticed that the gate had been left open. The prospect of running out of the farm to investigate was a very attractive one, and she made quickly for the gate. Suddenly she heard her name being called and turned to see the most beautiful woman she had ever encountered. She wore a long blue dress and had long blonde hair, and looked like Rapunzel in story books. 'You must not go through the gate,' the beautiful lady said. Nadine did as she was told. Now, as an adult, she realises that this was no ordinary lady.

Many things have happened that lead Nadine to understand that she has a special closeness with the mythical creatures of the other world. The most dramatic of these examples concerns a visit Nadine received from an ex-boyfriend. They were not getting on particularly well, and after some unpleasant words had been exchanged Nadine saw to her concern that he was very upset. It seemed odd that the slight altercation had made him distressed – he must have been feeling emotional she guessed. Suddenly she was aware of a figure sitting protectively next to this young man on the sofa in an attitude of concern. Nadine told her ex what she could see, but he was disinclined to believe her. She went on to describe this figure in great detail. He was wearing Doc Marten boots and a uniform of the type she had never seen before. It was obviously camouflage of some kind, but of a style and colour totally different from the usual army camouflage. Now, all of a sudden, Nadine's friend burst into tears. He sobbed for some time and when he finally managed to control himself told Nadine that the figure was that of his best friend and companion in the SAS. While they were fleeing a recent conflict, Nadine's ex had turned to see his friend running towards him. Before his eyes the friend was shot in the back and fell into his arms, where he died. Of course, this had been a traumatic experience. And now that he was distressed, his friend was right there beside him. His guardian angel was also in uniform.

★ ★ ★

It is also common to encounter a loved one as a guardian angel in near death experiences; indeed, people on the brink of death sometimes smile at the appearance of someone they recognise. In these cases it is frequently reported that the dying person will hold out a hand or stretch their arms wide to be taken to the next world. Some time ago I took part in a video about angels made for television. The video was introduced by Fiona Castle, wife of the much loved entertainer Roy, who used to present *Record Breakers*, but who sadly died of cancer. She explained how Roy Castle had heard beautiful music when nearing the end of his life. Eventually, when it was his time to go, he suddenly gazed towards the bedroom door, beaming with happiness because he could see Jesus. 'He is here,'

Roy told Fiona and his church minister, who was sitting at the side of the bed. 'I am to be taken to heaven at last.' With a wonderful smile on his face and hands outstretched, he died. There are, however, people who recognise their angels not because they are loved relatives who have gone on to the next world but because they are still very much alive.

It was the first time seventeen-year-old Amy had been out of Australia and she did not mind admitting that she was extremely nervous at the thought of travelling so far alone. Telling herself to 'get a grip', she hugged her mother goodbye at the airport and vowed not to be silly about the journey. After all, her sister – who, two years her senior, was working in Paris – would be meeting her at the other end. The journey was long and tiring, but after meeting her sister and her friends and getting a good night's sleep, Amy felt reassured – though, it has to be said, still rather timid. She was unhappy exploring on her own and always felt relieved when her sister could accompany her. Nevertheless, she had a great time and the month passed with frightening speed.

Next, she travelled on the Eurostar to London, where her aunt met her at Waterloo. She would be spending three days in London before flying back to Sydney and the end of her adventure. Her aunt was friendly and welcoming but expected Amy to be independent. Monday morning dawned, Amy was due to travel to the airport and her aunt had to leave early for work. Pointing out to Amy that the nearest tube station was just around the corner, she told her that she would easily be able to get to Heathrow on the underground. Off she went, and Amy almost collapsed in panic – she had expected to be driven to the airport and she had no idea how to accomplish this journey across a strange city. Her mind was blank with terror.

Huge snowflakes fall past my window as I write, and, looking out towards the moors, I marvel at how beautiful the day is. However, I don't have to go out this morning. I have just been chatting on the phone to Isabel. A native of Aberdeen, she is only too aware of the disruption snow can cause. This morning she was grateful that she did not have to attend a university lecture but could sit by the fire and study. Isabel has more reason than most for staying at home and keeping warm. From childhood she has been prone to chest problems. As a child she suffered from bronchitis and had to spend a great deal of time in bed when the winter was bitterly cold.

One year, when Isabel was just eight years old, a bout of bronchitis was so severe that the doctor was visiting daily and her parents were afraid that if she did not improve within a day or so, she would have to be admitted to hospital. Sitting with Isabel one night, her mother was very distressed to observe the condition worsen. She was convinced that when morning arrived, Isabel would have to be admitted to hospital. At one point she left her daughter's bedside to make her a drink in the kitchen. Suddenly a soft white light formed at the foot of Isabel's bed. From the centre of this light a figure gently emerged. Staring transfixed and not at all afraid, Isabel saw the beautiful face and shape of a traditional-looking angel. It was a face she would never forget as long as she lived. Then, slowly, this lovely creature faded back into the light and the light in turn gradually dimmed. Once more, the only illumination in the room, was a small lamp. 'I knew for certain I wasn't dreaming,' she says, and she recalls vividly telling her mother when she returned that she at last felt sleepy. This was very good news, because sleep had been fitful up to that point. Isabel fell into a deep refreshing sleep. The next morning everyone was surprised and grateful to see how much improved she was.

Isabel told her parents about the angel, but she could tell by their indulgent smiles that they did not believe her. Isabel, however, never forgot her angel. By the time she reached her teens, she was in better health and did not dread winter weather. She started a university course and, although her family home was not too far away, enjoyed sharing accommodation with friends. It was nice to have independence but also the knowledge that her family was on hand should she need them.

Returning to university after the Christmas break one year, many of Isabel's friends came down with a nasty bout of influenza. It was only a matter of time before Isabel also succumbed to the virus. She felt dreadful but decided that she was too ill to travel home and the best course of action was to stay in bed. Not wishing to alarm her parents, she simply did not ring home. They will assume I'm busy, she reasoned. During her second night of illness, Isabel thought that she had not felt so unwell since the days of her childhood bronchitis. I hope I won't have to go to hospital, she thought, shivering with cold yet overheating simultaneously. Then, as she reached for the glass of water by her bedside, she became aware of the room brightening. Turning to look at the foot of the bed she gasped. The light, now intensely bright, had a figure within its glow. It was her angel! As before, she felt no fear and marvelled at how beautiful the angel was. This, she was certain, was her guardian angel. Once again, the next morning saw a great improvement in Isabel's condition and the knowledge that she was going to be fine. Today she feels a wonderful sense of being cared for and watched over, and is happy in the knowledge that her angel will be with her for life.

Our next story begins in Turkey, with its warm sunshine and beautiful beaches, a favourite holiday destination for the British in recent times. Mary and her husband were looking forward to spending their honeymoon there. However, on reaching Ephesus, Mary began to feel very ill indeed. So intense was her pain that Mary was taken to hospital, where the doctors ordered emergency surgery for appendicitis. It was a terribly frightening and distressing experience for both Mary and her husband, who waited anxiously for her return from theatre.

Returning from the operating theatre, Mary recalls opening her eyes and seeing her husband asleep on the sofa next to her bed in the hospital room. It was at this point that something very extraordinary happened. Mary was suddenly prompted by an unknown urge to walk out of the room. Aware that she was naked, she rose from the bed, wrapped herself in a white sheet and stepped into the corridor. She recalls very clearly the feeling of the cold marble floor beneath her feet. At the door of the room next to hers she stood still and gazed inside. It was occupied by a man of about thirty years of age and wrapped in white robes. He sat up in bed, a drip attached to his right hand. Raising his left hand, palm facing Mary in a gesture almost of peace, he gestured towards her room – a clear indication that she should return to her bed. Turning, Mary walked back to her own room and climbed into bed, glancing as she did so at her still sleeping husband.

The next moment, however, she realised husband was not asleep but anxiously sitting by her bed willing her to wake. Moreover she was not naked. What exactly had happened? She was totally confused. Then she discovered that the room next to hers was in fact a staff room and there simply could not have been a man occupying it. Yet her experience was far more vivid than any dream she had ever experienced. Was this a vision, or an out-of-body experience? Of one thing Mary was certain, this was an event that would stay crystal clear in her memory for ever.

Years passed. Mary's marriage was happy, she had two small boys she loved dearly and a job she enjoyed. On one level, life was rosy, but Mary was finding life exhausting. Her position in a large hospital was high-ranking, and its demands were taking their toll. As a wife and mother she gave her all each day – mentally, physically and emotionally. Moreover, there were no family members close at hand to help her. She was beginning to feel stressed and exhausted.

This difficult situation came to a head one night. Feeling completely swamped by the pressures of work and family, she was at a loss what to do. In desperation she jumped in her car and simply drove, trying to clear her head. Some ten miles away from home, she found herself close by a lovely church. She parked her car, hoping to be able to sit in the church for a while and enjoy the peace and quiet. Finding it to be locked, she wandered into the adjoining graveyard. Her spirits at a very low ebb, she began to think of herself as a failure and quietly murmured into the darkness, 'Will somebody please help me?'

Mary returned home and went to bed – only to wake up some time later. Her husband was fast asleep beside her. Getting up, she wrapped herself in a white sheet and walked out of the bedroom. She walked to the end of the landing, noticing that the loft door was wide open. Underneath this door stood the very same man she had seen ten years before in far-away Turkey! The same face, with the same compassionate expression. He was shining a torch skywards, creating a beam of light. Then, once again, he made the familiar hand gesture to indicate that Mary should return to bed.

Could this really be just a vivid dream or was it a vision? One thing Mary feels for certain is that this was her angel guide, returning in a time of difficulty to comfort her. No one has waved a magic wand over Mary's life. Her problems still have to be faced, but – as she told me – the stress is a good deal reduced and she can see clearly the way ahead. She is certain that the right plan of action will present itself and all will be well. I'm sure she is right; how could it be otherwise with such a distinctive angel?

Letters reach me on a regular basis from all over the world. It is an astonishing fact that two will often arrive at the same time telling a story that is identical. I recently received not two but three almost identical stories, involving young girls approximately the same age, all of whom were rescued by a familiar figure. Here is Anna's account of her daughter's miraculous escape.

Lying in bed watching the early morning sunshine stream across the bedroom floor, Anna felt happy and contented. It was a beautiful spring day with deep blue skies, and to top it all it was a Saturday, so no one had to rush. It had been a stroke of genius to convert the large landing space into a play area for her little daughter, Chloe. Lots of toys and games were now stored there in boxes; it was a thickly carpeted and warm area, and there was a huge, glass skylight that flooded the landing with sunshine on fine mornings. Now Chloe was happy to play when she woke up, instead of arriving in her parents' bedroom at an unearthly hour. Anna could hear her now, talking to her toys.

Then, without warning, there was a deafening crash, shaking almost the whole house. There was no doubt about the location of this noise, it came from the landing. Sick with fear, Anna and her husband leapt out of bed and through the door onto the landing. It was difficult to absorb the details of the sight that met their eyes. The huge, heavy, glass skylight had fallen in one onto the floor. Shards of jagged glass and splinters of the wooden frame were everywhere. There was no sign of Chloe, who had certainly been playing on that very spot, only seconds before. Picking their way through the glass and wood as quickly as possible, they rushed into their daughter's bedroom. Sitting calmly in her bed, Chloe asked, 'What was the big noise?'

Anna and her husband took it in turns to hug their daughter, almost faint with relief. 'How lucky, darling, Anna said, that you decided to come back to bed.'

'Auntie Bea told me to,' Chloe replied.

Anna and her husband exchanged confused glances. 'Are you sure darling?' Anna asked her little daughter.

'Yes,' came the reply. 'She was wearing her lovely blue dress.'

Anna's Auntie Bea had indeed been wearing a blue dress the last time they saw her at Christmas, but she had died three weeks later. There was no doubt at all in their minds that their daughter would have been killed had she not moved from the landing. We can only thank Bea, they decided, for being Chloe's guardian angel.

Chapter 6

Listen to Your Inner Angel

★ ★ ★

We all have an inner angel, but mostly we choose to ignore it. This angel is that little voice that tries to protect us, alerting us to the presence of danger if only we can hear it. Richard Webster, in his book *Spirit Guides and Angel Guardians*, says, 'Like me you have probably heard the inner voice at times, heeded it occasionally and ignored it at other times.' He goes on to say that he always listens to it now, because he knows that his guardian angel has his best interests at heart. He adds, 'When I follow the advice of my guardian angel, I can't help do the right things and take the right actions.' We have probably all experienced this but may have chosen to dismiss it as instinct or imagination.

After the dreadful disaster of nine/eleven I read many moving stories in the press. A terrible number of people lost their lives that day, but many lives were saved by that inner voice. One young woman, realising that she had left at home some important papers that she needed for an early morning meeting in one of the twin towers, debated whether to return for them. The traffic was getting worse by the minute and she did not know what to do for the best – if she returned she would certainly be late for the meeting. But a voice inside, she said, urged her to turn back. Obeying, she turned her car around. The fifteen minutes it took her to reach her home and start out again for work saved her life. She would certainly have been in the building when the first plane struck. One man whose young son was starting school that morning, decided that he really wanted to take him on that special first day. He ignored the fact that he should have been in the office and followed the voice that told him to be with his son.

Ysanne was a girl who obeyed the voice – maybe because she was a sensitive musician and in every sense of the word tuned in. Because she was willing to listen, the inner voice saved her life.

On holiday in Israel one year, she was unaware that her much loved grandfather had died. She was enjoying a lovely holiday, wandering around soaking up the scenery and the history of Jerusalem. One day, particularly engrossed in her walk, she rambled into an unknown area. Narrow alleys fanned out on all sides and Ysanne, unconcerned, chose one to walk down. All at once, she heard a voice telling her not to choose that way. She glanced around, but there no one was in sight. She knew instantly that this was an inner warning and turned around. Minutes later she heard the dreadful sound of a bomb exploding and realised at once that it was on exactly the spot where she would have been had she not retraced her steps. Knowing that the explosion would have been reported in the news, later that day she rang home to assure her family that she was fine. That was when she heard the news that her grandfather had died. She had always been close to him, and he had been very protective towards her. There was no doubt in Ysanne's mind that he was protecting her still.

Gazing out at the miserable February weather, a holiday appeared to Clare's mother be an attractive proposition. She searched the internet for a bargain and had soon persuaded Clare's father that it would be a good idea to spend a week in the sun. Having booked the holiday, Clare's parents suffered a sudden stab of guilt at leaving their daughter alone. Trying not to sound irritated, Clare reminded them that she was actually nineteen and would be going to university later that year. She was secretly delighted at the prospect of having the house to herself – peace and quiet to study for her A levels and a night or two having all her friends around ... Packing complete, Clare's mother gave her lists of things to remember and safety warnings. After much reassurance and several goodbye hugs, Clare's parents finally left for the airport.

Clare loved her parents dearly of course, but she knew she would enjoy the space and freedom their absence would afford. The evening will be bliss, she thought. When I've finished studying I'll have a long warm bath, make my favourite dinner and watch all my favourite programmes. And that's what she did. Snuggling down in an easy chair in front of the television, she decided it would be lovely to light a few perfumed candles to complete the scene. She spent an enjoyable evening, and her parents rang to say they had arrived safely in Spain. Before going to bed, Clare followed the safety routine. She locked all the doors and windows, unplugged the television, blew out the candles and switched on the burglar alarm. Finally, she sank into bed and fell quickly into a deep sleep.

She woke with a start at the sound of her name being spoken very close to her ear. Switching on the light, she realised that there was no one there and she must have been dreaming. She lay down again, pulled her duvet up around her ears and hoped to go straight back to sleep. Again the clear soft voice said, 'Clare' – and this time there was the sensation of pressure on her shoulder. She switched on her bedside light, pulled on her dressing gown and got out of bed. The room was empty as before and the door firmly shut, but she realised that this was not a dream.

The house was quiet as she carefully and slowly made her way down the stairs. In retrospect she says it was incredible that she felt no fear, simply curiosity. On entering the lounge she was horrified to see smoke billowing from the armchair in which she had been sitting all evening. She seized a thick woollen throw from the sofa and threw it over the flames. Then she rushed to the kitchen, filled a plastic bowl with water and emptied it onto the chair, where the flames had speedily started to lick the chair back. Fortunately, the water effectively extinguished them. Clare stood trembling with fright.

'What on earth could have happened?' she said aloud. Mentally retracing her steps before bed, she vividly recalled locking the window beside the armchair, blowing out the candles on the window ledge and drawing the curtains. Somehow, she concluded, a still smouldering candle must have been knocked into the seat of the chair and eventually burst into flames. Wondering why the smoke alarm had not gone off, Clare checked the batteries and found that they needed changing. It did not bear thinking about what might have happened if she had not woken up. 'How fortunate I was to hear the voice of my guardian angel,' she tells anyone who will listen.

★ ★ ★

Fourteen-year-old Elizabeth was very interested in all things spiritual and always had been, even as a very small child. She was at a loss to explain why, because her family had no interest in such things whatsoever. She had never been taken to church or even read about such things as angels, but nevertheless she believed in both God and angels with a deep conviction.

One cold, foggy winter's day, Elizabeth's mother was feeling very unwell. As the day wore on there was little improvement and Elizabeth became quite worried about her. For a while now Elizabeth had been saving her money to buy a beautiful cross and chain she had been admiring for a long time in a shop window. On the same day she found to her delight, on counting her savings, that she finally had enough money to buy it. Braving the fog, she slipped out and bought the cross, then hurried home to show her mother. However, on her return she saw that her mother was a good deal worse, and she set off again straightaway to buy her mother medicine. There wasn't much time, because the chemist's closed at 4 pm, so, seizing the money for the medicine, she ran to the bus stop, fervently hoping the bus would arrive on time.

The bus ride took no more than ten minutes, but in that time the fog had thickened considerably. Alighting from the bus, Elizabeth realised with horror that she could not see the other side of the road that she would have to cross in order to reach the shop. The traffic sounds were muffled and she had no idea if any vehicle was approaching. She felt very afraid and yet she knew that she must hurry. Plucking up courage, she stepped out into the road. All of a sudden, a heavy hand was placed on her shoulder and a voice said, 'You must not go now,'

Elizabeth stopped in her tracks and was immediately aware of a car travelling so fast in the fog that it would have hit her for certain. With no idea where the voice had come from, she was initially shocked and frightened. There was obviously no one anywhere near her. But then she suddenly felt secure and warm. This lovely feeling spread from her shoulder, where the hand had been placed. She had a sense that there was a huge angel behind her, a positive behemoth of angels. She feels that not only did her guardian angel protect her that day, but that he is ever close.

Shrieks of excitement filled the corridor; girls hugged each other, some laughing, some crying – giggles and sobs mingling. There was a cacophony of noise. Lesley stepped into the corridor, her heart pounding. This was A level results day. Taking the long awaited and long dreaded results slip from her teacher, Lesley tried to steady her hand in order to read it. She had passed all three A levels, with good grades. She felt weak with relief.

Later that evening, when she had time to sit and talk to her parents, Lesley told them of her plan. She wanted to take a gap year before university. She intended to get a job, save the wages and then travel before settling down at university. In truth, her parents were half expecting this news. They agreed that if Lesley found a job and saved for the trip herself, then they would not try to dissuade her.

To Lesley's delight, she quickly found a job in a local garment factory. She would be a canteen assistant, helping to prepare breakfast and lunch for the workers. The wages were low, but she could walk to work in only 10 minutes, and her fellow workers were all very friendly. The one drawback with this job, however, was the early start time. Never an early bird, Lesley found this very difficult.

Weeks passed and Lesley was decidedly happy, saving assiduously and even adjusting to the early mornings. But then autumn arrived, and the darker mornings made it harder to leave the comfort of her warm bed. When winter came, and with it very dark mornings indeed, Lesley's parents became a little concerned about her walking to work in the dark, so Lesley's father began to accompany her to the factory door. The route they followed each morning departed from the busy main road down a side street, passing a row of derelict houses. In the eerie first light, Lesley found them decidedly spooky.

One chilly morning as they passed these houses, Lesley distinctly heard someone calling her name. Turning swiftly, she was surprised to find the street completely empty. Her father had heard nothing, making the incident stranger still. For three consecutive mornings, Lesley heard her name called. Deciding this was not an earthly voice, however, she was bewildered but not afraid. The voice was soft and gentle and quite unlike any she had ever heard before.

Lesley told her father that she wanted to walk to work another way. She felt that somehow the voice was a warning. He was happy enough to take an alternative route, even if it was slightly longer. When they arrived at the factory on the fourth morning, he was relieved that there was no mention of voices and happily left his daughter at the factory door. Minutes later one of Lesley's colleagues arrived, eyes wide with disbelief. It appeared that as she was driving her car past the empty houses, she had heard a great thunderous roaring noise. Braking swiftly, she looked behind her and saw several of the houses crash in a heap onto the pavement. Lesley felt a cold shiver run up her spine. Had she and her father not taken the alternative route that morning they would certainly have been walking past the houses at the precise moment of collapse! Suddenly she knew for sure the origin of that lovely voice. It had to be her guardian angel.

★ ★ ★

Judi drove to Heathrow Airport to meet her daughter, due on a flight from Singapore in the early evening. She was worried and confused to find that her daughter was not aboard the plane. She ascertained that her daughter had been on the flight when it touched down in Paris and tried to have her paged at the airport. Still no sign of her daughter, she thought hard about what should be done. Something told her to go and buy a ticket from Paris to London for her daughter, which she knew she wouldn't have enough money to buy herself. Approaching the nearest desk – Air France, as it happened – she asked for a single ticket from Paris to London on the next flight. 'Would you leave it at the Air France desk in Paris please?' she asked.

The woman behind the desk looked at her in complete bafflement. 'How will your daughter know it's there?' she said.

It did seem a totally impractical plan. Judi ran through the options in her head. Neither she nor her daughter had a mobile phone with them, and paging had not worked. Nevertheless, as she handed over the money for the ticket, Judi felt a calm certainty inside that this plan would work. Shrugging, the woman behind the desk arranged for the ticket in the name of Judi's daughter to be available at the Air France desk in Paris, commenting that she could not see how the girl could possibly guess it was there.

Judi went for a coffee and, checking the arrival time of the next flight from Paris, settled down to wait. They had been planning to meet relatives in London for dinner, so Judi calmly rang them to explain that her daughter would be on the next flight and they would be late. The arrival of the Paris flight was announced and Judi made her way to the arrival point. Sure enough, her daughter appeared, totally unflustered, and said simply, 'Hello, Mum.' Jumping into the car, they sped off to meet their relatives in London.

It turned out that Judi's daughter had taken travel sickness pills which had made her very drowsy. When the plane landed in Paris, waking with a start, she had assumed she was at Heathrow. She could not understand why everyone was speaking French! Her predicament had slowly dawned on her – not enough money for a flight home, no means of contacting her mother, other than paging her at Heathrow, which had not produced any response. Pausing for only a second, she had approached the Air France desk, which happened, by sheer coincidence to be the one nearest. 'Have you got a ticket for me?' she asked the Air France official, and was not in the least surprised when she said yes. Silently Judy's daughter said, 'Thanks, Mum.'

When they mulled the event over, it seemed like a minor miracle, and they wondered whether perhaps they had read each other's minds. Today, Judi concedes that their inner angels could indeed be responsible.

The art of intimacy is literally the art of the angels,
For it's the art of learning to fly beyond the
darkness of the world.

Marianne Williamson

The final three stories in this chapter feature angelic laughter rather than angelic voices. I'm sure that one of the angelic qualities is humour and that angels enjoy hearing us laugh.

One beautiful day in late summer, I was giving an angel workshop. As usual, when I finished speaking, I asked if anyone had any questions. To my surprise, a woman put up her hand and asked: 'Do angels have a sense of humour?' Without waiting for my answer she told the following story.

For some time she had felt that her life was lacking a spiritual direction, and she pondered where to find one. Eventually, she came across Reiki. Reading more about this ancient form of healing, in which spiritual energies are directed through the practitioner's hands to the patient, she decided that it might just be the answer, so she booked herself onto a weekend course to learn this ancient art.

She left work early on the Friday afternoon of the course and set off to drive to the venue with eager anticipation. This really is it, she thought. This is my chosen path and I'm sure the angels are guiding me. At that very moment a beautiful white feather drifted down towards her and stuck on the windscreen of her car. She could scarcely believe it. This surely was the sign. No doubt about it she was being guided by an angel to her chosen spiritual path.

As she drove along, more and more feathers appeared, all drifting towards her car. She was totally mesmerised. Approaching a sharp left bend in the road, she slowed down and carefully turned the corner. Directly in front of her now was a positive snow storm of feathers – emanating from a large lorry piled high with cages full of chickens! Laughing out loud, she decided there and then that angels have a sense of humour!

You don't have to study to become an angel – just wing it!

Nicole Beale

Helen grew up in beautiful north Wales. For her, living on a small-holding surrounded by a loving family, sheep and plenty of activity was a dream. She was specially close to her grandmother. They would chat happily together for hours and Helen loved her very much.

One spring, when Helen had not yet started school, her grand-mother became very ill and came to live with Helen's family in order to be cared for. Climbing the stairs to her grandmother's bedroom became a regular event for Helen. She would check to see if her grandmother needed anything or simply say hello. But as the days passed, Helen's grandmother became more seriously ill and the family tried to distract Helen from rushing up and down the stairs. Then the day arrived when her grandmother died.

The family thought it would be better if Helen was not involved in all the necessary arrangements, so it was decided that she would be taken out for the morning when the undertaker came to take their grandmother away. However, children often have a sense of things being amiss on these occasions, and as soon as she arrived home Helen rushed upstairs, past her mother in the kitchen, with a great sense of urgency to see her grandmother. Arriving at her grandmother's bedroom, she was puzzled to find it empty. Her head full of questions, she turned to go downstairs – and was surprised to be met by a man dressed completely in white, with snow-white hair

Helen recalls feeling very matter of fact and not at all fazed by this stranger. 'Who are you?' she asked.

'I am an angel,' he replied, 'and I have come to take your grandmother to heaven.' This all appeared to be perfectly logical to the little girl, who accepted it completely.

Calmly walking downstairs, Helen was met by her mother emerging from the kitchen. Gently she began to explain to Helen that her grandmother had died. 'I know,' said Helen brightly. 'I just met an angel upstairs and he told me'. Her parents exchanged puzzled glances but were relieved that she was clearly not distressed.

A little time elapsed and the family was thrown into the hurly-burly of lambing. One morning Helen skipped into the field to find her father bending over a lamb that had just died. Turning to Helen, he said, 'The little lamb will be in heaven now with your grandmother.'

'Oh good,' Helen replied. 'Grandma loved roast lamb. She will be having lamb and mint sauce for dinner tonight!'

If you have ever offered to wash up the dishes without being asked, you may have found yourself being accused by your mum or dad of having an ulterior motive. Lisa's mother smiled to herself when her daughter rushed to tackle a large sink full of washing-up after a family lunch. She was smart enough, however, to say nothing until the task had been completed.

Sitting in the lounge with a cup of coffee, she listened carefully as her daughter asked if she had heard about the Mind, Body and Spirit festival that was going to be held in town soon. 'Yes,' replied her mum. 'Why do you ask?' Lisa explained that she and her best friend, Alice, were very keen to go and she wanted her mother's permission. Lisa's mother was pleasantly surprised, for she had fully expected Lisa to ask if she could go to some rock concert or other, miles away from home. The catch proved to be the cost. The entrance ticket together with fares and meals for the day amounted to a much larger sum than Lisa's allowance. But Lisa's mother gave her permission to go, plus an advance on the following week's allowance.

Bright and early on Saturday morning the girls joined the queue outside the hall where the festival was being held. They were totally unprepared for the sights and sounds and smells that greeted them as they walked through the door. Drums, bells and singing filled the air. Scented candles and joss sticks made a heady mix, and the girls thought it all quite wonderful. Lately, Lisa had become fascinated by angels. She had read my book *Angel at my Shoulder* and secretly wished that she too could be visited by an angel. She bought books, jewellery and cards depicting angels. It was a very full and enjoyable day for Lisa and Alice.

Arriving home, Lisa was full of her day out and wanted to tell her mother all about it. Excitedly she started to talk about what she had seen, but her mother stopped her, saying, 'Dinner's ready. Have a wash quickly, and tell your father to come – then we can listen while we're eating.'

Lisa did as she was told, urging her father to hurry. Leaving the garage, where he had been fixing a security light, her father smiled and hurried indoors. It was lovely to see his daughter so enthusiastic and he listened intently to her news. At the end of the meal, Lisa asked her parents if they thought she had a guardian angel. Her mother answered that she felt certain that she did.

Lying in bed that night, Lisa went over the events of the day. Her thoughts turned again to the subject of angels and how they had appeared to many people all over the world, and she drifted off to sleep pondering on her guardian angel. Some time later, she woke with a start. Her bedroom was flooded with light. Catching her breath she sat up in bed and wondered if this was it. Would her angel appear in this light? Minutes passed but no angel appeared and the light did not change in density. Puzzled, Lisa left her bed and went to her bedroom window. Opening the curtains she realised that the bright beam of light was actually the new security light her father had fixed to the garage. Someone must have activated it! Fortunately, Lisa has a good sense of humour and started to giggle. Climbing back into bed she wondered if her guardian angel was also laughing!

★ ★ ★

We all have an angel within us, and the ability to exercise it. You will probably be familiar with the expression 'What goes around, comes around'. When we perform an angelic deed – an act of kindness for others – it does not simply vanish into a black hole. It ripples on, and one day returns to you. If we look for the angel within others, they will also see the angel within us. Listen to your inner voice and let your own angel see the light.

Go out and do a random act of kindness
Then say, 'My angel made me do it.'

Sally Sharp

Chapter 7

The Angel Thread

Angels are everywhere. They manifest their love through every heart, every honest smile, every act of kindness, every constructive thought. Their signature is in everything that grows, every selfless desire, every playful pirouette of every soul. They are always trying to reach you through music, art, drama and the written word. In sunshine, flowers and rain, there is always an angel trying to communicate with you.

Karen Goldman

In this chapter I hope to show how many facets of our lives are linked to the angels – for we are connected to them in every way imaginable. We can see their presence in nature and hear it in music; we can smell their beautiful fragrance; we can identify angels in deep inner feelings and dreams. Angels contact us not just by appearing before us; in fact, seeing a full-blown angel with wings and bright lights is pretty rare. However, if we look closely at our everyday lives, we will discover that we have all had angelic experiences. Who has not been part of a happy coincidence or a moment of serendipity, felt a warm glow of love, had a special dream or marvelled at a carpet of daffodils in spring? You may not associate these experiences with angels, but believe me they are connected. The more you look for angels in the world around you, the greater the possibility of recognising their presence. It's all about creating a bridge for them to cross into your life. The following stories will, I hope, help you to see just how many areas of life have the angel thread running through them.

Abby was miserable. In all her seventeen years of life, she declared, she had never felt so bad. She had cried herself to sleep and eaten large amounts of chocolate, but nothing helped. Her mother tried hard to make her feel better, but Abby told her that nothing could ease the pain of being dumped!

It was a harsh, ugly word, but it summed up the situation succinctly. She was in love and she thought Mark was too, so it was a huge shock when he told her, none too gently, that they were finished. School had just ended for the summer and Abby had been looking forward to spending time doing things with Mark. Shutting herself away in her bedroom, she said out loud, 'If only Gran was here.'

Abby's grandmother had died some twelve months previously. She and Abby had been close, and Abby had felt able to chat to her about anything. Abby's grandmother would have known instinctively what to say and what not to say. She would simply have listened for as long as it took. She was greatly missed by all the family, and especially by Abby.

Fiona was Abby's best friend, and she had been very supportive. At this point the day was getting pretty hot, so when Fiona arrived and suggested they go for a swim, Abby agreed. Exercise, Fiona said, was good for the spirits. She turned out to be right, and as Abby swam length after length, she felt the tension leave her. Emerging from the swimming pool tired and relaxed, Fiona had her second brainwave of the day. She steered Abby to their favourite coffee shop and ordered two big slices of chocolate fudge cake. Laughing, Abby tucked in, admitting that the cake, although not as good as her grandmother's, was nevertheless delicious.

For the first time in several nights, Abby slept well and woke feeling optimistic. She was instantly aware that she had dreamed about her grandmother. She marvelled at the dream's clarity. In it she was walking through a beautiful garden, in which she found her grandmother sitting on a bench. In her hands she held a bunch of wonderful flowers. They were huge and unlike any Abby had ever seen. The colours were unusual and the flower heads a strange shape. Her grandmother smiled and handed the flowers to Abby.

'It was so clear, Mum,' Abby said as she related the dream to her mother over breakfast. 'I can see the flowers in my mind's eye still.'

'It was your gran telling you that she knows you're sad, she cares about you still and she hopes the flowers will cheer you up.'

Changing the subject, Abby's mum told her that her aunt in London had rung the night before. 'She said she was sorry to hear about the end of your romance. She knew how keen you were and how important the relationship was for you. She sends her love and told me to tell you that life will be happy again, sooner than you can imagine.'

It was good to be surrounded by people who cared for her and loved her, Abby thought. Later that morning, while Abby and her family were drinking coffee in the lounge and chatting, there was a ring on the doorbell. Abby's brother answered and came into the lounge carrying a large bunch of flowers. They were for Abby, from her aunt in London. 'How sweet of her!' said Abby's mum, but Abby could only stare speechlessly.

'Whatever is the matter?' Abby's mum asked.

'These are exactly the flowers Gran gave me in the dream,' Abby replied. 'I've never seen any like them before.' She stared at the long-stemmed flowers with their multicoloured heads.

'No,' said her mum, 'I don't suppose you have. They're not terribly common, because they have to be imported. They're called birds of paradise.'

'Well, there you have it,' said Abby's father. 'What other flower would Gran have in heaven?'

Hush my dear, lie still and slumber,
Holy angels guard thy bed,
Heavenly blessings without number,
Gently falling on they head.

Isaac Watts

A divorced mother of two boys, Joanne was now happily remarried. One night Joanne had a dream about her first husband's father, who had died a year ago. In her dream she saw him waiting in a taxi. Clearly anxious to go somewhere and to attract her attention, he smiled at Joanne and waved his hand. Shortly afterwards, Joanne had another dream, and again it was very clear and atmospheric. This dream featured a large church, its exterior walls covered in large, brightly coloured flowers. Joanne stared, having never seen such wonderful blooms on a church wall before. Next, Joanne was led into a house with large interior connecting doors. The dream was so vivid that Joanne could not get it out of her head but it did not seem to make any sense. Then Joanne had another dream. This time the main character in the dream was her ex-husband and he was standing in an antique shop. It all seemed very odd to Joanne.

Soon after these dreams, Joanne received a phone call from her ex-husband. He wanted to have the children to stay with him for a couple of weeks. He asked Joanne if she would drive them to where he now lived, Chertsey, in Surrey – a place she had never visited before. Arriving in Chertsey, she could scarcely believe her eyes. There before her was the large church of her dream – it was in fact Chertsey Abbey – and the exterior walls were covered in the most unusual bright flowers. How weird, Joanne thought, I've never been here in my life, but that's definitely the church in my dream. Collecting her thoughts, she followed the directions she had been given to her ex-husband's house. Here another surprise awaited. Inside the house, the large distinctive connecting doors were exactly the same again as those in the house in her dream. Finally – yes, you've guessed it – an antique shop exactly the same as the one in her dream could also be found in Chertsey. Struggling to make sense of all this, she decided that this journey was clearly intended and the visit in some way significant.

Some days later, when Joanne was back home again, the phone rang. It was Joanne's ex-husband. He told her that he had to return to Scotland to scatter his late father's ashes and asked if she would agree to him taking his sons with him. At last Joanne had found an explanation for her strange series of dreams. She believes that through them her ex-father-in-law communicated with her, ensuring that she would agree to her boys visiting their father and accompanying him to scatter their grandfather's ashes. It seemed it was his wish to have his family together for a final goodbye.

> No one with an unbiased mind, can study any living creature however humble, Without being struck with enthusiasm at its marvellous structure and properties.
>
> **Charles Darwin**

'Do you think you could possibly sit down for a moment please,' said Joyce's husband, as he watched Joyce bustling around the room. Life was always busy for Joyce. She was interested in so many things and enjoyed social occasions so much that her husband called her 'butterfly'. Then friends and family adopted the name. She tells me it's because she flits about from one thing to another; however, I think there is another reason too, for she is very pretty and extremely colourful in her dress.

A trip to a lovely hotel in the seaside town of Llandudno was an annual treat for Joyce and her husband. This year they were particularly happy when they returned to the news that they were going to be grandparents. The baby arrived and the christening was planned for late autumn. Joyce and her husband looked forward to this day with great excitement. Their first grandchild and all the family gathered to celebrate – it would be simply wonderful. With the day fast approaching and all the arrangements finalised, however, tragedy struck. A few days before the christening Joyce's husband died.

The whole family was devastated. The christening was postponed and replaced by a funeral. The family struggled on through a winter that was bitter cold and grey. Finally, after Christmas, the christening was rearranged. As she left for church, Joyce pulled on her warmest coat, knowing only too well that no matter how hard the old boiler tried to heat the place, the church was always cold.

The small party made its way to the font, the proud parents followed by Joyce. It felt strange not to have her husband by her side, and she thought to herself as she walked, I wonder if he can see us. Without warning, a tiny shape fluttered down in front of Joyce's face and landed directly at her feet. It was a beautiful butterfly! Aware that her mother had stopped walking, Joyce's daughter turned around. She could scarcely believe it when she saw the butterfly. Joyce picked it up and placed it carefully on a window ledge, a warm glow spreading all around her.

How on earth could a butterfly appear in the depths of winter in a bitterly cold church? Joyce had the answer. It was a sign that her beloved husband was with them after all.

There is a sequel to this story. When spring finally arrived, Joyce was gripped with the desire to go once more to the hotel in Llandudno where she and her husband had spent so many happy holidays. Although it would probably be painful at times, she felt that there she would feel closer to him. She arrived at the hotel in wonderful sunshine, and after unpacking made her way to the dinning room for lunch. She chose a seat by the window, marvelling at the spring sun shining on the sea. Her heart felt warm too, as all the memories came flooding back. I must be brave, she thought. I have to make a life for myself and be grateful for all the happiness I have had. 'Am I right?' she silently asked her husband. 'Will I have the strength to carry on?'

The answer arrived instantly, in the shape of a large and beautiful butterfly. It fluttered directly to where Joyce was sitting and landed on the windowsill next to her arm. 'No mistaking that message!' she said with a smile.

I looked up butterflies in a book about the symbolism of the natural world. It said, 'The butterfly is a positive symbol, standing for the powers of transformation, and immortality. It is beauty arising from apparent death.' Need I say more!

We move from butterflies to birds in our next story. Margaret loves nothing better that to walk in the countryside and by the sea. She is fortunate to live within easy reach of both. Bird watching is one of her hobbies and her favourite bird is the buzzard. Without realising why, she felt greatly drawn to these birds. She began to see them more and more often when she was birdwatching, and started to wish that she could hold a buzzard. Hardly believing it possible, she asked the angels if they would make her dream come true.

Not long after Margaret had spoken to the angels, she and her husband visited Bodelwyddan Castle. To her delight, in a large marquee in the grounds a man was displaying large birds of prey. In his hands was a huge buzzard. He instantly picked Margaret out from the crowd and beckoned her to come and hold the bird. Trembling with excitement, Margaret moved forward and pulled the proffered gauntlet over her hand and arm. The man started to tell Margaret and her husband all about this particular bird, adding that he had problems with his vision. 'Well, so has Margaret,' replied her husband.

'They must be soulmates,' said the bird handler.

Suddenly the buzzard flapped its huge wings and stared directly into Margaret's eyes. She felt a sense of pure elation, peace and awe. She was at one with this huge creature and it was such a powerful experience that tears streamed down her face. The wings of the buzzard felt like the wings of an angel to her at that very moment. Her angelic prayer had been answered.

★ ★ ★

Joe and Simon definitely did not enjoy family gatherings. Birthdays and Christmases, when all their relations gathered together, were for them a trial. Nevertheless, they were very fond of their Aunt Margaret. She did not have a family of her own and when they were children would make a fuss of them when they visited. Passionately fond of gardening, she had a beautiful garden and the brothers loved to play cricket and croquet on her spacious lawn. They had happy memories of hot summer afternoons followed by tea out in the garden, and the smell of night stock filling the garden always reminded them of their aunt.

They felt very upset when Aunt Margaret died. The hot summer afternoons seemed very distant on the bitter winter day of her funeral. Margaret was their mother's sister, and she was particularly sad at her loss. Sitting over a cup of tea that evening, they all told stories of Margaret and talked about how fond they all had been of her. The boys commented that of all their relatives she was the one they particularly liked. Their mother seemed pleased and a little easier in mind as they all made their way up to bed. As they reached the landing, Joe turned with a strange look on his face. 'Can you smell anything?' he asked the others.

'Night scented stock,' said his mother with surprise.

They all stared at each other, and then Simon said in a matter-of-fact voice, 'Goodnight, Aunt Margaret!'

And I saw another almighty angel come down from heaven
Clothed with a cloud: and a rainbow was upon his head.

Revelation 10

Is there anyone who doesn't love the sight of a rainbow? People often tell me how a rainbow appeared at the very moment they need reassurance or when they were missing a loved one. Robert's story reminds us of how the rainbow connects us to heaven.

It had been six months since the death of Robert's father. He says it had been the longest six months of his young life. Struggling to adjust to life without his dad was bad enough, but now he had to prepare to leave home for university. Originally this prospect had filled him with excitement, but now he was worried about leaving his mother alone and leaving behind all the familiar sights and objects that brought his father close. The garden where his father had spent so much of his time was filled with memories. How could he bring himself to leave so soon after his death? The day of Robert's departure was very emotional. He vowed to be strong for his mother's sake, though inside he felt anything but strong as he gave her a goodbye hug. His uncle lifted Robert's suitcases into the car and gave him a kindly smile as they set off.

It would be a drive of several hours, and for most of that time Robert was silent, lost in his thoughts. His uncle respected this and concentrated on the driving. At last they arrived. Robert carried all his belongings to his room. The hall of residence was very quiet, not many students having arrived yet, and Robert felt very strange and alone as he waved his uncle goodbye. It was late afternoon by now and the rain that had been falling steadily during the drive finally ceased. A walk to get his bearings seemed like a good idea, so Robert went outside to the grounds of the hall.

The surrounding countryside was pretty, and at another time Robert would have felt very pleased with the location. Walking down the long drive he kicked the pebbles with considerable force – it felt a little better to vent his grief on them. Turning at the end of the drive to walk back in the direction he had come, he found himself wondering if he would ever feel better. Then, looking up, he was taken aback by a rainbow suddenly forming in the storm-dark sky. He caught his breath, for it was huge and dazzlingly beautiful. For the first time in weeks, his spirits lifted. 'I will cope,' he said to himself. 'Dad is never far away, just the other side of the rainbow.'

You may be thinking that rainbows appear to everybody all the time, so how then can they be so special? The significant thing about rainbows – or any other symbol come to that – is the timing. Take Linda's story for example. She wrote to me from Cumbria to tell me the story of her ice rainbow.

Linda had never quite seen eye to eye with her mother-in-law and this became most evident one Christmas, when they had a disagreement about arrangements for the festival. Going for a walk to nurse her grievance, Linda followed a path covered in ice.

As she approached a bridge, she caught her breath, for the sun had come out, making the ice underneath the bridge radiate a huge rainbow. She felt her mood lift and pondered on the important things in life. She knew that she had to settle her differences with her mother-in-law. She felt that she was being guided to do this by angels manifesting in the beauty of nature, and she was thankful for this message. Not long afterwards, her mother-in-law died, and Linda realised just how important it had been to make her peace.

Linda sent me a photograph of the ice rainbow, and it is indeed breathtaking. However, when I looked at it, I thought that what Linda wanted me to see was the ice angel under the bridge. Then I spoke to Linda, and it was evident that she had not in fact seen the angel that had simply jumped out at me. Looking at the photo again, she saw the angel clearly, ice wings outstretched under the bridge. So do look with care when out walking – otherwise you may just miss your very own angel!

* * *

I recall several years ago a large advertising initiative to encourage people to buy more flowers. The slogan was simply 'Say it with flowers'. Be they red roses on Valentine's day or forget-me-nots, flowers have the power to speak volumes. A lovely little story involving African violets illustrates how plants and flowers can bring messages to us.

Beryl had never felt very close to her mother and found her very hard to talk to. Another regret in Beryl's life – of less importance, but still it made her sad – was that she had trouble keeping plants alive. There was nothing 'green' about Beryl's fingers whatsoever. Her favourite plant was the African violet. Time after time she would buy a wonderfully healthy specimen, only to have it die on her. She sadly concluded that for her African violets were simply not to be.

Towards the end of her mother's life, however, Beryl found that they were becoming closer. She looked after her mother during her last few months, and their relationship at last appeared to be easy. Then her mother died and lots of practical things had to attended to, including sorting out her possessions. Picking up a box full of belongings one day, Beryl noticed a marvellous African violet in her mother's bathroom. It was full of dark purple flowers and Beryl loved it. 'I'll put it in my bathroom,' she told her family, 'but I know only too well that it won't last long.'

Months passed and the African violet was hanging on, but when the winter came and the violet flowers died, Beryl feared the worst. February arrived and her mother's birthday was approaching. To Beryl's total amazement the plant suddenly burst into life, filling the bathroom with wonderful purple flowers just in time for the special day. Beryl was delighted that the plant had survived the winter. How odd, she thought, that it had flowered on her mother's birthday. The flowers bloomed for several weeks before once more dying.

Early summer was lovely that year. As Beryl looked out into the garden she realised that the anniversary of her mother's death was approaching. So imagine her amazement when she went to the bathroom and saw the African violet once again in full bloom. First her mother's birthday, now the anniversary of her death – it really was amazing. A remarkable coincidence, you may think, but the fact is that every year since the plant has bloomed twice yearly on exactly on those occasions. I looked up purple violets in my book of flower symbols. It gave as their meaning 'forever in my thoughts'.

The visible world is made to correspond with the invisible and there is nothing in this world but is a symbol of something in that world.

Abu Hamid al-Ghazzali

The most common way in which angels communicate with us is one that we have all experienced at one time or another – namely coincidences. You are walking down a street thinking about a friend or relative. Seconds later there they are in front of you. You fully intend to get in touch with someone you have not heard from in a long time and before you can do so a letter arrives. We simply say 'What a coincidence!', but look a little deeper and you may discover a that there's more to it than meets the eye. A series of 'coincidences', some of which proved to be life-saving, are the focus of our next story.

As a young man, Frank joined the merchant navy. At one point, he was home on leave and preparing to return to his ship the following day. In order to do this, he had to catch a bus at midnight, but he was running late, so he hurried as best he could with a large, heavy kit bag on his back. Then, just as he was approaching the bus stop, he looked up to see his bus speeding down the hill. There was absolutely no way he would catch it now, and dropping his kit bag to the ground, he let out a huge sigh of frustration.

It was not the end of the world, however. There would be another bus along in a while, though it would be too late for Frank to make all his connections. Eventually, another bus hove into view, and Frank climbed aboard. The bus went down the hill and around a steep bend and then suddenly slowed. In front of them was a serious accident – a vehicle had crashed and completely turned over. It was the bus Frank should have caught. He decided that a guardian angel had definitely been looking after him that night.

Some time later Frank was due to board another ship due to sail for Canada. It was carrying timber from Great Yarmouth across the Atlantic, and the voyage would take twenty-one days to complete. Feeling a sudden and inexplicable great urge to go home, Frank decided not to enlist on the ship and, following his heart, went home. During the voyage there was a dreadful storm and the ship, with everyone on board, was lost. Could this be my guardian angel again, Frank thought, and I'm sure he knew the answer.

Frank's final experience during his career at sea involved another storm and an old lady. The storm arose in the early hours of the morning, and the ship was rolling dangerously. A little old lady in her cabin rang the bell for attention. She was so tiny and frail she was having trouble staying in her bunk. Each time the ship rolled, she was afraid of being thrown to the floor and injured. Frank said he would help, and, finding extra pillows, he wedged her into the bunk, then pulled the bedclothes tight, effectively pinning her in. There was no way she could fall out, he thought, or even get out without assistance. The old lady had also noticed that her cabin porthole was leaking due to the severity of the storm. With a tool specifically designed for the task, Frank tightened the porthole. It was now leak-proof and certainly could not open.

The ship sailed on and the storm continued. Only a little while later, Frank was surprised to hear the old lady's bell again ringing for assistance. The sight that met his eyes when he entered her cabin was nothing short of astonishing. The little old lady was out of her bunk and peeping through the porthole, which was wide open! Just how this was possible Frank could not imagine. Climbing out of her wedged-in position would have been hard enough, but to open the porthole without the necessary instrument was impossible. 'I certainly couldn't have done it,' Frank told me, 'never mind a frail little old lady!' His amazement did not stop there, though. The lady told him that a figure had appeared in the cabin as if from nowhere and told her not to be afraid. 'The storm will soon go,' it had said. Frank was lost for words. This time, though, it must have been the old lady's angel!

Frequently a coincidence involves a dream, always extremely lucid and staying vividly in a person's memory. The following dream and the subsequent events were experienced by my daughter Gillian.

A cat lover, Gillian owns a beautiful marmalade puss called Peaches and for some time has wanted to add another cat to the family. The new cat would be especially welcomed by Peaches, she thought, who usually spent her days alone while Gillian and her husband were at work. One night Gillian had a very lucid dream about a cat. Every detail was clear and distinct. The cat was black and white, with most unusual markings. Four white feet, a white tail and a white chest stood out against the jet black of the coat, and there was a cute white flash on the cat's nose. On waking Gillian told her husband about this dream that had made such an impression on her. He said, as did all her friends, that she just had cats on her mind, having just decided to obtain another one.

Two days later, Gillian was preparing to visit a friend who lived a considerable distance away. It was very unusual for her to drive such a long way alone and she was a little uncomfortable at the prospect. She was particularly anxious about getting lost. Well, she got to her friend's house OK, but at one point in her journey home, she was suddenly horrified to discover that she really didn't know where she was any more. As she was on the motorway, she could hardly stop to check the map and now her worries were suddenly compounded by a loud noise from underneath the car. Exiting the motorway as soon as possible, she drove in search of a garage, but the noise was by now so loud that she pulled over to the side of the road to investigate. The exhaust pipe was hanging off the car and needed urgent attention.

Gillian was in a panic. She was completely lost on a suburban road, no garage in sight and no friend or family within range. If she rang her husband she would be unable to tell him her location and her car was in no fit state to be driven in search of signposts or garages. She was, she says, 'stressed out'! On the verge of tears, she was suddenly distracted by the sound of a cat meowing in greeting. Turning, she saw a cat exactly like the one in her dream, walking down the garden path of the nearest house to meet her! It even had the distinctive white flash on its nose. Delighted, and forgetting for a moment her troubles, she bent to stroke this beautiful friendly cat, at once feeling all tension leave her. A smiling couple now walked down the garden path. They clearly owned this lovely cat. Engaging them in conversation, Gillian told them of her dilemma.

Hardly believing her ears, Gillian felt relief flood through her as the man said, 'That really isn't a problem. I can to fix the exhaust for you.' In no time the car was ready to go, and the couple gave her clear and concise directions home. 'How amazing was that?' Gillian asked me. 'Do you suppose guardian angels arrive in cat form?'

'It certainly wouldn't surprise me in the least,' I answered.

Angels can appear in other forms,
Even as animals to protect us from harm.

Anon

I've come across many angel stories in which objects play a central role. Indeed, even very mundane objects sometimes take on a heavenly connotation. This is the case in our next story. Would you believe it? The object is a milk jug?

Since she was a child, Susan had loved the little sugar bowl and milk jug her mother used. She would borrow it to play house with her friends. When Susan was only twenty years old, her mother died. What made matters worse was that Susan had been working in Australia at the time and did not even get to say goodbye properly. It was not until about a year later, when the family house had been sold and all the fixtures and fittings had been dispersed, that Susan recalled the little milk jug. No one, it seemed, could remember it, despite her detailed description. 'It had pictures painted around the edge of black and white cows,' she told her family, but her brothers had no recollection of what had happened to it. Sadly, Susan gave up, concluding that perhaps it had been broken at some time.

At the age of twenty-six, Susan was engaged to be married. She had a house of her own and was gradually buying things to make it cosy and attractive. As the wedding day approached , Susan's thoughts turned to her mother. She deeply wished her mother could have been at her wedding and felt quite tearful as she busied herself with the preparations.

A week before the big day, Susan was visiting her chief bridesmaid, who lived some 50 miles away in a small, Lancashire market town. They had fun walking round the market stalls, buying locally made cheese and fresh fruit. Stumbling upon an antique stall, they stopped to look at the intriguing items. Susan suddenly let out a shriek that made her friend jump. 'Whatever is the matter?' she asked.

'I've found my mother's milk jug!' she answered, with eyes like saucers. And, indeed, there was the sweet little jug with its black and white cow decoration still fresh as ever.

She asked the stall holder where the jug had come from but she had no idea. 'I must have had that for years,' she said. 'It's been sitting in box at the back of my garage for ages.' Buying it for only a small amount, Susan lovingly placed the jug in her handbag. She would no doubt receive many wedding presents the following week but none would be more precious than this.

The angels send us what they deem we can cope with. Our final stories involve the most dramatic manifestation of the angel thread: powerful heavenly signs often involving light and, on rare occasions, the actual appearance of an angel.

Lynne, from Shaftesbury in Dorset, kindly gave me permission to share her very moving story with you. Her dearly loved dad was dying and had entered a hospice. He faced his final days with courage, supported by his family and his strong spirituality. His birthday fell while he was in the hospice and the family shared the rather sad task of helping him celebrate it. They were all too aware that this birthday would be his last.

Lynne had noticed that her father's cross and chain, usually beside the bed, were missing. The chain, he told her, had broken, and in order to keep it safe, he had wrapped it in a paper tissue. Perhaps it had been mistaken for rubbish and thrown into the waste basket. The loss upset him as the cross had brought him a lot of comfort over the years. 'I'll buy another for his birthday,' Lynne told her partner, and together they drove into the town to find one similar.

As Lynne waited by the car for her partner to buy a parking ticket, she was suddenly overwhelmed by the most wonderful perfume. There was no rational explanation for this, and she felt in her heart that the angels were confirming that they approved of what she was doing. Sure enough, she found a perfect replacement cross and her father was touched by the beautiful gift.

All too soon, Lynne's father began to fade and everyone knew that the end was very close. The family – Lynne, her mother and one of her brothers – gathered at the bedside. Her youngest brother found the occasion too difficult and felt that he could not stay. In the early hours of the morning, something amazing happened. Around Lynne's father's head and shoulders there appeared a bright, glowing light. They knew that this light was taking his soul to heaven. Each member of the family sent their love with him into the light as he slipped into the next world. Suddenly the light had gone, and with it, said Lynne, her father's spirit. The family felt blessed to have witnessed such an amazing sight.

Since that time, in autumn 2002, Lynne has had other indications that the angels are very near, but she and her family will never forget witnessing the light literally from heaven.

Nothing can ever separate you, not even death,
As long as you continue to love.

William Swinfield Thaw

For the past five years Hannah had been the star of her school's highly successful netball team. Fleet of foot, she played in the centre and could always be relied upon. In all the time she had been on the team, she had not sustained a single injury – until now that is! A simple fall, or so it had first appeared, was followed by a sickening crack as the bone in her leg broke. It was not an ordinary fracture. She was going to need to have a pin placed in her leg.

She lay in hospital after the operation feeling sorry for herself and wondering how long it would be before she could play netball again. As Hannah was now sixteen years old, she had been placed on an adult surgery ward. The ward was very busy. Women of all ages filled the beds, and for the most part were very friendly and nice to Hannah. One woman, in the bed directly opposite, was especially friendly. She was recovering from an ankle injury and was nearly ready to go home.

As Hannah sank into a deep sleep at the end of her second day in hospital, her family tiptoed away from the bedside, hoping that she would be in better spirits the following day. Some time later, Hannah woke feeling slightly disorientated and wondering if it was morning, although it appeared still to be dark. A figure was making its way along the ward, pausing at the foot of each bed as it did so. It was surrounded by a soft, white light. As the figure approached Hannah's bed, she recognised the woman from the bed directly opposite. She must be going home, Hannah decided. The woman smiled and moved on, continuing to visit each bed. Finally she reached the end of the ward, where she gently pushed open the double doors and disappeared.

Aware of a certain amount of activity in the ward, Hannah asked a nurse what was going on. 'Nothing dear,' she replied. 'Go back to sleep' and, almost instantly, Hannah did. Later when, the daylight and activity of a busy ward woke Hannah, she recalled the events of the night before. Why, she thought, was the lady opposite going home in the middle of the night? Her bed was now empty, and Hannah asked the nurse why the woman had gone at such an odd hour. Startled, the nurse asked what she meant. She was equally startled by Hannah's response: that she had seen the woman walking down the ward, stopping at each bed to say goodbye. Gathering herself, the nurse said gently, 'It must have been a dream, Hannah. Sadly, the lady in the opposite bed died during the night.' It turned out that she had developed a blood clot without anyone being aware of it. Although she was only young, the clot had proved fatal.

Hannah is convinced that she was not dreaming. What she saw was far too clear and distinct, she says. That woman really was saying goodbye and the light was taking her to heaven.

Interestingly in this connection, Dr. Hans Moolenburgh, the Dutch doctor and angel researcher whose story is related earlier in this book, told me a lovely piece of Hebrew lore. According to this lore, no doctor should stand at the foot of a patient's bed, as that is the place for the angels. An interesting belief when you consider how many stories refer to angels appearing at the foot of the bed.

★ ✶ ★

People frequently ask me how they can tell if they've seen an angel rather than a ghost. After all, many angel encounters feature figures dressed in everyday clothing. I tell them exactly what the hundreds of others have told me: when you see or feel the sensation of a ghost, the atmosphere is one of fear. The temperature drops, you may feel very cold, and the room remains dark. An angelic presence, on the other hand, emits a sense of love and comfort. It produces no fear, and the atmosphere is one of warmth and light. Our next story illustrates both these phenomena. It also illustrates the fact that asking for help from an angel can sometimes have dramatic effect.

Many of you will have seen the film *The Sixth Sense*. It is the absorbing and moving story of a little boy who sees spirits. He eventually overcomes his fear and asks the spirits why they come to him. Finally he understands that it is because they need help from him in order to progress to the next world. You might think that this is a sweet but far-fetched story, but you would be wrong. It seems that it is not uncommon for people who have died to be grounded, as it were, by some problem here in this world and to need some sort of help to move on. It is in these circumstances that a church exorcist is sometimes called upon. But sometimes a willing, spiritually attuned person can also provide the help that is required. Much to Angela's surprise, she became one such helper.

For some time, Angela had been aware of a very cold spot in her dining room. Even when the rest of the room was as warm as toast, this cold area remained. Why this particular place should be so cold was a complete mystery to her. The dining room was long and L-shaped, and open into other rooms. There was nothing in its layout that yielded an explanation. It was a weird anomaly that the family had just decided to live with.

The situation became much clearer, however, when Angela joined a spiritual awareness group whose members had the ability to pick up on the presence of spirits. Angela told the group about her dining room cold patch wondering if they could shed light on the phenomenon, and a group member said she would be happy to visit the house and investigate.

As soon as she entered the house, this woman was aware that there was in fact a spirit present. Using her ability to communicate with spirits, she began to ask it questions. It appeared that this was a man who had been a farm worker in the area where the house now stood. The house had actually been built on farmland years ago. The man said that his little daughter had drowned in a pond on the site of the house and he was waiting for her. Gently the helper suggested that, through a form of meditation, she should ask the angels to take him on his way, but he would not consider this at all and said that he could not possibly move on without his daughter.

It seemed that there was little anyone could do about the situation. Angela continued to live with the cold area, but was troubled by the fact that help had been refused. One evening at the group meeting Angela was told that members of the group could see a little girl sitting at her feet. This did not disturb Angela at all – indeed, she thought it very sweet. Several meetings passed, and the little girl was always at Angela's feet. By now Angela was becoming spiritually aware herself, and she began to be able to feel this presence. She experienced it as the lovely sensation of a child holding her hand. What all this meant she had no idea. It was only some time later, when a group member suddenly said, 'I think your farm worker is here, Angela,' that the penny dropped. Could this be the little girl that the farm worker had lost –his much loved dead daughter? It all began to add up. Angela was the link and both the man and the little girl had been drawn to her, hoping for her help.

The group decided to meditate, hoping to send both father and daughter on their journey with love. It had taken Angela some time to get the hang of meditation – not an easy practice, as anyone who has ever tried it will tell you. However, on this occasion, meditation came easily and Angela was able to visualised the little girl and the farm worker clearly. They were holding hands, smiling broadly and waving to her. Then she saw them leaving a cave and going into the light. At that point she felt a tug at her shoulders, as if she were being held back. She was not to go any further. At last, father and daughter were reunited, and were leaving the dark place they had been in for the light.

As soon as she arrived home that evening, Angela rushed to the dining room to the area of the cold spot. It had gone! How amazing, she thought, that I have been the catalyst for this spiritual reunion. My thought was, how amazing to hear of a person helping an angel instead of the other way round. Mind you, with a name like Angela, perhaps we should not be surprised!

Michelle remembers her fifth Christmas vividly. The first shiny parcel she opened was exactly what she had wanted so badly: a doctor's kit. With great excitement she lifted out the toy stethoscope, plasters and bandages, declaring emphatically that when she grew up she was going to be a doctor. Her family smiled indulgently and submitted themselves to being bandaged for the rest of Christmas. Laughing at the memory, Michelle told me that even the cat didn't escape. She ended up having to have a plaster cut from her fur!

Michelle's fascination with all things medical grew, and today she is a medical student in a large teaching hospital. As she hopes to specialise in paediatrics, she was delighted to find herself working on a children's ward recently. One night a little girl called Emily was brought from surgery into intensive care. She had been in a car accident and was very poorly indeed. The whole team treating her was terribly concerned. Standing by her bed in the hours after surgery, Michelle found herself praying, 'Please, God, help this little girl.' The hospital had all the latest technology and a highly competent, dedicated staff; nevertheless, Michelle felt that in this case some extra help would not go amiss. But Emily was a fighter and slowly she began to improve. Her weak little smile became stronger by the day, and Michelle began to feel a real rapport with her.

The day arrived when Emily was sitting up in bed and smiling broadly at everyone. It would only be a matter of days before she could go home once more to her relieved family. Michelle knew that she would miss this little ray of sunshine. At the end of one of her shifts, Michelle dropped in on Emily, knowing that when she returned from her short break, the little girl would have been discharged. As Michelle sat by the side of her bed, Emily announced, 'I have something for you,' and handed Michelle a colourful drawing. It was easy to see that the main figure in it was Michelle in her white coat with her stethoscope around her neck. The identity of the second figure, however, was a mystery.

'Who's that?' asked Michelle. 'Is it the nurse?' To be honest it did not look anything like a nurse.

'It's the lovely lady who used to come with you to see me,'

Emily replied. Michelle looked even more confused. 'You know, the one in the beautiful white dress, very pretty and with a light on her head.'

Michelle looked again at the picture and a shiver of excitement ran down her spine. She knew exactly who the other figure was, it was Emily's angel. God had indeed answered her prayer for extra help for this special little girl – he had sent one of his angels.

As I have already mentioned, a full-blown angelic encounter is comparatively rare. Much more frequently, as we have seen in this chapter, we are contacted through nature or music or through the eyes of children. There are occasions, however, when the sight of an angel is exactly what is needed, and there are people who are not at all fazed by an angelic appearance. The following stories relate some of those rare encounters with angels in all their splendour, the first one in the most unusual location.

Asked where you think might be the most likely place for an angel to appear, what would be your answer? A church or a graveyard perhaps? We can easily imagine angels in a dramatic biblical setting – such as the angel Gabriel appearing to Mary to tell her of the amazing events to come, or the heavenly host singing on the hillside before the shepherds on that first Christmas eve, or the angel with the flaming sword showing Adam and Eve the way out of Eden. We can picture perfect settings for such angelic apparitions in our mind's eye. But I bet the last place you would imagine an angel appearing is in a supermarket. Against all odds, however, this is the case in our next story. It's proof, if proof were needed, that angels are as relevant and as close to us today as they were thousands of years ago.

Patricia has worked in Tesco for many years and, as you can probably imagine, it's a very busy job. When you're working on the tills non-stop for several hours, it's nice to know that a break is coming up. One particularly busy morning found Patricia longing for a much needed cup of tea. At last a colleague stopped by Patricia's till and announced that it was time for a break and that they could go together. Rising from her seat, Patricia joined her friend and they walked off together chatting happily.

Most supermarkets, of course, have many tills in a row, and the two women had to walk past all of these to reach the staff recreation area. Suddenly, just as they reached the very end till, Patricia was stopped in her tracks, for there, standing behind a very good friend of hers who was working busily away, was a huge angel! Opened-mouthed and incapable of speech, Patricia could only stand and stare. She estimated the figure to be at least 8 feet in height, and it was clothed from head to toe in soft, flowing, white garments. Behind the angel, his wings were neatly folded above his head, making him appear even taller. It was an awesome sight.

Puzzled, Patricia's companion realised that her friend was no longer walking alongside her and asked what on earth the matter was and why she was standing still. It was evident that no one else could see this marvellous being, and Patricia felt very privileged and not at all disturbed – simply astonished. It was evident to her also that this angel was there specifically for her friend, so busy at her till and totally unaware of this special visitor. The angel was leaning protectively towards her, but Patricia had no idea why. One thing was clear, though: she would keep this experience to herself, for she knew very well that her friend at the till was distinctly nervous about all things spiritual. Saying nothing about the matter to anyone, Patricia composed herself and went calmly off for her break.

Shortly after this incident, Patricia's friend was absent from work due to illness. After tests were completed she was, sadly, diagnosed with cancer. A tumour had to be surgically removed and, shortly after this procedure, Patricia visited her friend. By now it had become crystal clear to Patricia why the angel was there, for he was obviously protecting her friend. She also now understood why she had been the one to see him: she was meant to tell her friend about the angelic presence now that the right time had arisen. Convinced that this angel was there to heal, she told her friend the whole story, together with her own interpretation of the event. The light on her friend's face was wonderful to see, and Patricia knew that she had done the right thing to tell her.

Now her friend also had something to tell Patricia. After the diagnosis she had, of course, been extremely distressed. The one place she had found comfort and solace was, strangely enough, on her stairs at home. Hanging on the wall there was a picture of a white dove, but viewed from the angle of the stairs it appeared to be an angel.

The dark days are behind now, and Patricia says that her friend is no longer afraid. What a wonderful location for a wise and caring angel to appear, and how right he was to let Patricia be the one to witness him.

I sit on the seventh step a long time
And I am sure the angel is there.
I tell him all the things you can't tell your mother and father.

Frank McCourt

Margaret could scarcely believe her ears. She stared open-mouthed at her daughter, Sara. 'Say that again slowly,' she requested.

'We are getting married,' Sara repeated in a steady determined voice.

Sitting down with a bump, Margaret said she thought her far too young. Sara and her boyfriend, Daniel, were both only nineteen years old. Daniel was studying at university and Sara was working in a job she loved, at least 200 miles away from him. None of it made any sense to Margaret, who voiced her objections forcefully as soon as she had recovered from her initial shock.

Sara went off to make some coffee and then sat down beside her mother to break the final part of the news: there was a baby on the way. 'I need something stronger than coffee,' Margaret said, turning white.

The days that followed were confusing to say the least. When both families had absorbed the news, they decided to have a conference. The two young people had made up their minds that they wanted to be married and nothing could dissuade them, and eventually both families decided that they would support the marriage plan. It was decided that Sara would leave her job and join Daniel in his university town. A flat would be found and the families would assist with finances until the young couple could support themselves.

Many tears and hugs later it was all arranged, and a small but happy wedding took place. Margaret worried a great deal about Sara being so far from her family while expecting her first baby. However, Sara was very well and managed to find a job for a few months to help out with the rent on the flat. Daniel was working hard at university and passed his second year exams with flying colours. Maybe everything will be fine after all, Margaret thought. Perhaps I'm worrying unnecessarily. 'They're far more capable than I gave them credit for,' she told her husband.

August arrived, hot and steamy. Sara finished her job in order to rest for the final month before the baby was due. Daniel was enjoying his summer break and said he would have time to help with the baby before he had to return to his studies. In the meantime, the heat was troubling Margaret and she could not sleep. After having lain in the dark for what seemed like the entire night, she decided to get up and make a drink. As she sat up in bed and reached for her slippers, she suddenly became aware of a light in the corner of the bedroom. It grew in intensity until the whole room was filled with light. Unable to move and scarcely able to breathe, Margaret stared in disbelief. Slowly in the centre of this light there appeared a figure, a traditional-looking angel in every respect, with a flowing white gown, long blonde hair and huge wings outstretched above his head. All her apprehension and fear evaporated as Margaret took in this wonderful vision. Love filled the room powerfully and all at once Margaret understood. It must be Sara, she thought. Something is wrong.

Waking her husband with difficulty, she urged him to get dressed quickly. She rang her daughter but was alarmed to find that there was no response Now she was sure that they must go immediately.

It would take them several hours to reach the town where her daughter lived, so from time to time she called her from her mobile. At last, when they were almost on the outskirts of the town, Margaret's mobile rang. It was Daniel. Sara had gone into early labour and he was with her at the hospital. Could they come as soon as possible? he asked. He was astonished to find that they were in fact only moments away.

Arriving at the hospital, they rushed to the maternity unit to find that Sara had just given birth to a baby daughter. The baby was small but the staff did not envisage any severe problems. A short stay in hospital until she was a little stronger was all that the baby required. Sara was tired but perfectly well. Tears of joy spilled from Margaret's eyes.

Some time during the following day, when everyone had settled down a little, Sara asked her parents, 'Why did you drive down during the night, without even knowing what was happening?'

When Margaret told her what had happened, Sara gazed from her mother to her baby daughter in awe. All she could think of to say was, 'Gosh!'

'You have no need to worry about your little girl,' Margaret said. 'She has her very own guardian angel!'

Epilogue

I hope that the true stories in this book will have persuaded you that the angels are very close to us and that they can play important roles in every aspect of our lives. This is perhaps especially true of their connections with young people who are beginning to make their own way in the world. It can be very reassuring to know that you have a special guardian watching over you and that all you have to do is believe.

We humans are the angels' intermediaries, through whom they can channel their energy and love to earth. Meet them halfway and ask for their help; tune into them and you will receive. You can do this through meditation, for example by sitting silently in front of a candle and concentrating on the flame (but remember never to leave a lighted candle unattended). Empty your mind of everyday clutter and let your thoughts come and go like clouds in the sky. If you hear it that little inner voice, the voice that belongs to your intuition, then listen to it – it could be the voice of your guiding angel.

Take a closer look at life's coincidences and you will find a deeper meaning and perhaps a direction. See afresh the world of animals, birds and nature in general, as a natural sign may contain a message meant just for you. Let music speak to you – if a certain melody or song is played at a significant time for you, it is probably a significant communication.

As these many and varied stories show, angels surround us, offering help and comfort all around the globe, from tiny nudges to dramatic appearances. They are certainly there for you too. Since the most ancient of times right up to the present day we have been helped by angelic influence. Believe, trust and thank heaven for angels.

Further reading

Anderson, Joan Wester, *Where Angels Walk* (Hodder and Stoughton, 1995)

Bloom, William, *Working with Angels, Fairies and Nature Spirits* (Piatkus, 1998)

Crosse, Joanna, *A Child's Book of Angels* (Barefoot Books, 2000)

Goddard, David, *The Sacred Magic of the Angels* (Samuel Weiser, Inc., 1996)

Goldman, Karen, *The Angel Book* (Simon and Shuster, 1998/1992)

Heathcote-James, Emma, *Seeing Angels* (Blake Publishing, 2001)

Heathcote-James, Emma, *After Death Communication* (Metro Publishing, 2003)

Moody, Raymond, *Life After Life* (Rider, 2001)

Moody, Raymond with Perry, Paul, *Reunions: Visionary Encounters with Departed Loved Ones* (Warner Books, 1995)

Moolenburgh H.C., *A Handbook of Angels* (The C.W. Daniel Company, 1984)

Reid, Lori, *Dream Magic for Teenage Dreamers* (Rider, 2002)

Resources

Zodiac Zone
(Angel crafts, books, jewellery and gifts)
PO Box 7007,
Hook,
Hants. RG27 8JP
Tel: 01252 843265

The Angel Connection,
(Mail order catelogue of angel artefacts)
White Stone House,
Grange Paddock,
Mark,
Somerset TA9 4RW

ANGEL
(Angel books, gifts and crystals)
PO Box 344
Manchester M60 2EZ

Moston Complementary Health Centre
(Angel sculptures and books)
282 Moston Lane,
Manchester M40 9WB
Tel: 0161 682 2733

Details of Vinni Medley's CD *Forever Young* are available on the web from *www.Botchit.com*
All proceeds from this music go to charity.
For details of Mee's music, see *www.Mee.mu*

If you have had an angel experience and wish to share it with the author, please contact her care of Rider Books, Editorial Department, Random House, 20 Vauxhall Bridge Road, London SW1V 2SA, or email her at glennyceeckersley@hotmail.com

Also available from Rider by Glennyce Eckersley

Order further Rider titles from your local bookshop or have them delivered direct to your door by Bookpost

☐	*An Angel at My Shoulder*	07126 72087	£6.99
☐	*Children and Angels*	07126 70777	£6.99
☐	*Angels and Miracles*	07126 12033	£6.99
☐	*Saved by the Angels*	07126 12173	£6.99

Free Post and Packing
Overseas customers allow £2.00 per paperback

ORDER:

By Phone: 01624 677237

By Post: Random House Books
c/o Bookpost
PO Box 29
Douglas
Isle of Man, IM99 1BQ

By Fax: 01624 670923

By email: bookshop@enterprise.net

Cheques (payable to Bookpost) and credit cards accepted

Prices and availability subject to change without notice.
Allow 28 days for delivery. When placing your order, please mention if you do not wish to receive any additional information.

www.randomhouse.co.uk